How to be Productive and Action-Oriented

BE GREAT TODAY

Foreword by Todd Durkin, Bestselling Author
of *The IMPACT Body Plan* and *The WOW Book*

JUSTIN KEGLEY

No part of this publication may be reproduced, stored in a retrieval system, or transmitted in any form or by any means—electronic, photocopying, recording, or otherwise—without prior written permission, except in the case of brief excerpts in critical reviews and articles. For permission requests, contact the author at justin@movementfitnessrockford.com.

All rights reserved.

Copyright © 2019 Justin Kegley

ISBN: 9781091159433

The author disclaims responsibility for adverse effects or consequences from the misapplication or injudicious use of the information contained in this book. Mention of resources and associations does not imply an endorsement.

This book is dedicated to my amazing, incredible, incomparable family.

To my brilliant, amazing, smoking-hot wife, Theresa. You are my ROCK! Thank you for always supporting me and pushing me to be my best. Without you, I would be lost. I'm grateful GOD made you mine forever. I love you to infinity and beyond!

To my boys Riley, Cooper, and Colton. Thank you for inspiring me and pushing me to be my best. I want you to dream, believe and achieve your true hearts' desires. May this book be a small piece to show you that with GOD anything is possible.

Table of Contents

Foreword by Todd Durkin 1
Be Great Today 5
Chapter 1: Wake Up Call 11
Chapter 2: Wake Up on Purpose 33
Chapter 3: Take Responsibility and Choose to Be Great 45
Chapter 4: Be Specific 51
Chapter 5: GO! 61
Chapter 6: Getting Accountability 67
Chapter 7: Focus 73
Chapter 8: Living with Intentionality 91
Chapter 9: Choose Your Attitude 101
Chapter 10: Choose Your Actions 109
Chapter 11: Go to Bed! 117
Chapter 12: Nutrition 139
Chapter 13: Get Moving 149
Chapter 14: Take Action: Now 157
The 28-Day Plan 177
Day 29 and Beyond 268
Acknowledgments 273

Foreword

ONE SAYING I COINED many years ago was, "Live a life worth telling a story about."

I believe that we ALL have a story to share.

I believe that we ALL have greatness within.

I believe that we ALL have MORE strength and power than we think.

I believe that we can all DREAM bigger and create way more IMPACT than we can possibly imagine.

So, let me ask you this …

What's your story?

Part of my life's purpose has been to "motivate and inspire millions to greatness and create IMPACT every day." That's what makes me tick. That's what fires me up. That's what gets me up early in the morning and lights a fire under my step.

What about you? What are you pursuing each and every day?

Maybe your purpose is:

- To be a great parent by offering your children the gift of your time.
- To give back to your community through philanthropic activities.
- To do well in school, in sports, or the game of life.
- To inspire greatness in your clients, co-workers, family, and friends.
- To create IMPACT physically, mentally, emotionally, and spiritually for the people whose lives you touch.

I believe it's important to be dedicated to a meaningful purpose in life and to live it every day. But experience has taught me that a life purpose isn't so clear to everyone. Some of you might be confused about exactly what you want to do. Or maybe your work doesn't align with your interests. Maybe you feel like you haven't had the right opportunities yet. Or, maybe you haven't CREATED the right opportunities for yourself … yet.

If you're asking yourself those questions, then you have come to the right place!

Justin Kegley has had a meteoric rise in the fitness industry. He and his wife, Theresa, are examples of what I call "fire-breathing dragons." They lead a team of five people at their incredible gym, Movement Fitness (Rockford, Illinois). They coach over 200 athletes and fitness enthusiasts there per week and inspire many more than that with their growing influence. They are the parents of three amazing children and value the parenting role more than anything. And they both are committed to deeply creating IMPACT and living a life worth telling a story about.

I have had the awesome privilege of being a mentor to Justin over the past three years. His drive, determination, passion, positivity, and commitment to greatness is extraordinary. His vision is big, and his heart and work ethic match his dreams. He truly is a man of IMPACT.

In your hand, you are holding a book that describes the passion and incredible story that Justin Kegley is living. As you read, you are going to learn about the strength he found within himself to get better, to dream bigger, and to create impact in his life and in the lives of everyone around him.

Better yet, not only is he going to share his secrets of success with you, he is also going to give you the exact plan to follow in order for you to create your own impactful life story. As you read, you will be inspired to step up, to get moving and to **BE GREAT TODAY**… and every day!

I encourage you, like Justin, to discover your purpose, then go out and use your gifts to make a difference in the lives of people

Foreword

around you. As you craft the most amazing story you can imagine, you truly will live a life worth telling a story about.

Peace and love,

Todd Durkin, MA, CSCS
Owner, Fitness Quest 10
Under Armour Training Team
Head Coach, Todd Durkin Mastermind Program
Author, *The IMPACT Body Plan* and *The WOW Book*

Be Great Today

MY FATHER-IN-LAW IS A wonderful man who is generous, loving and wise. He is fueled by his passion for faith, family and farm. He is outgoing and takes a genuine interest in everyone he meets. He is someone that I admire and try to emulate daily. If you call his phone, he has this voicemail that is warm and inviting, making you feel like he really means what he is saying. When I started my career in corporate America, I used the exact same voicemail, changing only my name and company. It says, "Hi, this is Mark Schleder with Midstate Ag. I'm sorry that I can't get to the phone right now but if you leave your name, number and a brief message, I will get back to you just as soon as I can. Thank you very much and have a great day!"

The last part of his voicemail began a stirring in my head about ten years ago.

HAVE a great day.

At the time, I was working for the pharmaceutical company Merck. I began discussing this thought with a colleague of mine.

He and I were both interested in motivation and how to maximize our potential. We talked about the beginning of this phrase. Not to split hairs or be the word police, but is *"Have a Great Day"* the best thing we can say to someone when we leave them? Is there something that is a little more specific? While it is well-intentioned, you can't always ***HAVE*** a great day.

Think about it.

Have you ever had a bad day?

Have you lost a loved one, a job or an opportunity? Has your car broken down, are your kids pushing every last button or has a friend turned their back on you? Ever had one of those days that just makes you want to crawl back into bed? *Yeah, me too*. Everyone does. The point is, you can't always *HAVE* a great day.

So, my friend offered the following idea as a replacement. "Why don't you tell people, ***MAKE*** it a great day!"

That sounds good. It's action-oriented, causes people to think about greatness, and drives a purposeful discussion. My question, though, is that we can't always ***MAKE*** something happen. We can't make other people see things the way we do. We have disagreements with our spouses, bosses and friends about our differences of opinion. We can't make other people work or see our vision and that can cause difficulty.

After some thought, I offered this. How about "BE Great Today?" The "BE" part is specific and is something we can do

ALL the time, if we choose. In all scenarios, we can choose to BE great. In the good, bad and in between, we control our attitude and our actions. We can make a choice in each moment, to be in charge of the things we think, say and do. I first learned this process through my faith. In a letter to the Romans, Paul wrote, "Do not conform to the pattern of this world, but be transformed by the renewing of your mind." (Romans 12:2 [NIV]) This means that being intentional, holding every thought captive to see if it is worthy of pursuing or thinking about is a choice we can make.

This is not easy. It will be an uphill battle, but if you want to transform your life, then you have to go uphill. You have to live intentionally. Choosing to be intentional about everything requires time, effort and change. It requires that we think first about our purpose, passion or mission, prioritize the most important and take action. It requires that we change.

Change is a big, hard and scary word for some. You might be thinking, "I've tried everything, and it didn't work," or "This is just the way I am." I don't believe that. I *BELIEVE* you can change your life, because I have and so have many others. But you first must change your thoughts in your head. You have to change your state of mind in order to implement strategies that will allow you to make a transformational shift in your life!

It is going to require that you have passion, purpose and live your life on a mission. It means that you are going to have to make sure that the thoughts in your head are true, not some made-up story of how you are or should be living. Make sure the life you are living is true to you and not for someone else. You have to be clear about what it will take for you to BE Great. Not just being organized in your calendar, but organized in your head, heart, soul, and body.

What do you stand for?

What are your priorities?

What is your purpose, passion, or mission in life?

Who do you want to become?

What does the "BEST" version of your life look like?

I believe we were all created to live a life that is abundant. Often our thoughts about abundance go straight to finances but I want you to have more than that. I want you to be rich in the spiritual, emotional and physical aspects of your life as well!

This book is designed to motivate and inspire you, while also giving you the tools to start taking steps forward TODAY! Author John Maxwell says that in order to have true transformation, "You have to move from good intentions to good actions." Well, that is exactly what we are going to do. You are going to:

1. Discover your purpose
2. Set your intentions
3. Establish systems to help you succeed

     a. Build your calendar

     b. Get accountability

     c. Set deadlines

4. Start taking action today!

Life is precious. I believe that you were created by a GOD that loves you and made you to be a light, shining bright for all to see. You were created with a purpose. I believe that He calls us to be transformed every morning. That means that each day, when we wake up, we need to focus our attention on things that are positive and excellent. It means that we have a chance to live on purpose, knowing that He loves you.

Today, start taking advantage of every moment in order to live your best life and to leave a legacy that impacts generations. Choose to be intentional with your Attitude and Actions so that you can wake up and Be Great Today.

Chapter 1

Wake Up Call

"I opened two gifts this morning. They were my eyes."
— Unknown

296 POUNDS!

I couldn't believe it! I knew it wasn't going to be good, but when I stepped on the scale at my in-law's house on Christmas, it read 296 POUNDS!

Growing up, I was an extremely athletic kid. I was the kid that always had a ball or bat in my hands. I played basketball, baseball and football. I started working out when I was 12 and had LOVED all of it. I competed in bodybuilding and powerlifting after my sports career in college football was over. I knew how to be healthy and keep myself in good shape.

Chapter 1: Wake Up Call

But somehow, I had let it all go. It started going downhill when I was a senior at Illinois State University. As a senior, I was focused on building job opportunities and connecting relationships that would help me in the future. I was the President of the American Marketing Association on campus, an organization of 150 students that had just won the Chapter of the Year Award. I started an internship at Wells Fargo which provided 15-20 hours of work per week. I was also serving as a bouncer at a bar three days per week with shifts that got me home at 2 a.m. I was working out five-six days per week, generally at 5:00 a.m., in addition to having my 15-hour class load. To say I was busy was an understatement. I was burning the candle at both ends.

My 5 a.m. workouts were done in bodybuilding style to keep up with the other meatheads on campus. We worked out at Gold's Gym in Bloomington, Illinois. There was a group of five-six guys that trained together. At the time, everyone in that group was interested in putting on as much muscle as possible. In fact, they were so interested that most of them took steroids to do it. It wasn't a path that I wanted to take, so I just tried to keep up with them naturally. Of course, we ATE! I put on 30 pounds thinking that the more I put on, the more it would eventually turn into muscle. Unfortunately, that is not how the body works, so, instead, I ended up having more body fat than I wanted.

Up at 5 a.m., finishing the day too late most of the time, I was wearing myself down and getting sick. Something had to go. That ended up being the training.

I was able to finish out my senior year and graduated from Illinois State University with a double major in Marketing and Human Resources Management in May 2005. Once I graduated, I began working full time at Wells Fargo. It was a good job that provided me with a very nice base salary, and since I had done an internship, I was able to hit the ground running. Right away, the company moved me and a friend of mine to Schaumburg to work. While I didn't love the job, it was a good opportunity with a company that provided a significant opportunity for growth.

After I moved, my lack of working out continued. I tried multiple times to correct it, but nothing really stuck. To go along with that, I was really enjoying my new freedom. The combination of a job I didn't love, with extra time and a little bit of money made for a dangerous combination. It meant eating out most nights of the week, drinking way more than I should and not exercising. It was a perfect recipe for weight gain, and did I ever pack on the pounds!

I lived that way for about six months.

By GOD's grace and a Jimmy Buffett concert, I rekindled an old relationship that never actually ended. Theresa was more than just an ex-girlfriend. We dated for over four years. Our families were close. My siblings were hers and hers were mine. Her brother, Caleb, and I held backyard trampoline wrestling matches with belts and everything. I went on family vacations with them, and we thought this relationship would progress at some point. She

Chapter 1: Wake Up Call

was the love of my life, that I thought got away. (Her brother was so mad at her when we broke up, he didn't talk to her for a month!) We just went in separate directions. When you are 1,000 miles away, a long-term relationship is extremely difficult, especially when you are young. She was off chasing her dream as a marketing manager at the Walt Disney World Company, and I was finishing school at ISU. She was passionate about what she was doing with her life, and I had just started a career.

After our initial breakup, we didn't talk for a while, but honestly, I thought she was still the one for me. Over time, we began talking about once a month, just checking in on each other and our families, but nothing more. This became a period of tremendous growth for me.

The biggest difference in my life was that I became a follower of Jesus Christ around this time. I had friends that invited me to Northwoods Community Church in Peoria, Illinois. I was at a place that changed my life. I grew up Catholic and had parents that stressed the importance of faith in our lives, but I had never developed a personal relationship with GOD. At Northwoods, Pastor Cal Rychener showed me the love of Jesus and the grace to know that even through all of my mistakes and faults, he would love me anyway. Plus, he lifted weights, and that was huge for me. I also met a mentor there named Randy Shafer who showed me what it meant to love other people no matter what, because that's the way Jesus loved us. My time at Northwoods built a foundation for my faith that has grown over time, and it became extremely important for me as I went to Illinois State.

Going to school at ISU was integral for my development as a person and as a leader. It challenged me to become the person I was meant to be. No longer satisfied to live an average life, I was striving for more. I became a better communicator, cared more about people, and learned so much throughout that time. It became evident to Theresa that I was a different person as well.

The freedom that a job and moving to Schaumburg provided allowed for new opportunities. One night, I got a phone call from Theresa saying that she had been in a car accident. Her car was totaled and while she was physically okay, she was emotionally wrecked. She was also disappointed because her friends from Florida were traveling to Chicago to see Jimmy Buffett at Wrigley Field. So, two things happened. First, I was able to help her with her new car purchase and second, I convinced her to fly to Chicago, stay with me and go to the concert. She did. And it changed EVERYTHING. We had an amazing weekend, and it was a huge first step for us. In fact, it was so great that two weeks later, she came back up and visited me and her sister at a Cardinals/Cubs game at Wrigley Field. Dave Ramsey wouldn't be happy with me because of the amount of money I spent then and the debt that I accumulated because of those trips, plus the subsequent ones I took to Florida. But it was worth every penny.

Chapter 1: Wake Up Call

We dated pretty much in secret, not telling family and only a couple of friends for months. After a few months of that, I got another phone call from Theresa. She asked me to come to Florida a couple of days earlier than planned for a trip. She was late and wanted me there with her to take a pregnancy test.

Whoa; things just changed. We had talked about me potentially moving to Florida to be closer to her, but nothing was working out. I couldn't find a job or housing that would fit. So, while I was going to Florida, I received word that I was up for a huge promotion with Wells Fargo. When I got to Florida, I went to Walgreens and picked up a pregnancy test … or three. She took the test and there was a pink vertical line very distinctly shown, but the horizontal one was not so distinct. We decided to call the company to ask for clarity, to which they kindly replied what I had suspected–the test was positive.

THE TEST IS POSITIVE?!

So, now we were in October of 2005, sitting in the Disney World Magic Kingdom, trying to figure out what to do. We knew that we wanted to be together. That wasn't a question. The first thing was to wrap our heads around the fact that we were having a baby! There's a stigma with that. We were Christians. This isn't how it was supposed to be. What would our families, friends, co-workers think? What would GOD think? What were we going to do now?

First, I can tell you, GOD's grace is good and sufficient, even in our faults. I know that because Theresa and I have been blessed in unbelievable ways in our marriage. I also know that because of the gift we have, a twelve-year-old boy who is such a blessing to our lives.

Our family and friends were incredibly supportive! They loved us and helped us in amazing ways, then and now.

Because of my promotional opportunity in Illinois and a lack of prospects in Florida, it became clear very early on that the best plan of action was not going to be for me to move to Florida. Plus, our family was all in the Central Illinois area. The clear, but very hard, reality set in. Theresa was going to be leaving her dream job and moving to Rockford.

On Christmas, 2005, we told our family and friends that we were dating again, getting married and going to have a baby. I will never forget the reactions, love and support we received then, and the joy we felt from everyone when we told them we were back together.

In January of 2006, Theresa left her job at the most magical place on earth, and I moved to Rockford, Illinois for my new position. It was a great opportunity for me, and also a tremendous blessing for my new family. On February 25, 2006, Theresa and I were married. What I once thought was not possible, rekindling this old flame, was now realized through our marriage and a soon-to-be growing family.

Chapter 1: Wake Up Call

That was an incredibly busy year for us. Along with the marriage, promotion and moving, we welcomed our first child, Riley, on July 19, 2006.

Throughout that year my eating habits went from bad to worse. Because Theresa was now pregnant, I obviously felt the urge to support her with late-night popcorn, ice cream or whatever else she "needed." Mostly, it was me continuing poor habits. We stayed up binge- watching "24" until midnight or later, having no regard for working out, eating well or doing anything that resembled being healthy.

Honestly, I tried to lose weight. Multiple times throughout the previous two years, I thought, "I need to lose 50 pounds." I would do the "New Year's Resolution Diets," or the "Everything Changes on Monday" plans, only to be continually disappointed. If you are unfamiliar with those plans, they go something like this:

*Commit to yourself that you will never eat bad again.

*Cut out every sweet or good tasting thing in your life.

*Work out really hard for a couple weeks, see little progress, get discouraged, quit and eat yourself into a coma because it doesn't matter anyway.

It's hard to get motivated when you feel like you are working hard, making huge sacrifices and the scale doesn't move, or moves very little. So, you give up.

After Riley was born, we kept the same patterns going. I would go to work, come home, spend all night with Theresa and Riley, staying up late, watching some TV shows, eating crappy snacks and hitting the snooze button in the morning, hoping to postpone the day a little. I went through one or two more feeble weight loss attempts, but life was all about finding a new "normal" after a year of rapid change. While I was unhappy with myself, I wasn't unhappy enough to make a significant change.

So now, at my in-law's house for Christmas, standing on the scale, I could see it.

296 pounds!!!

I had no words. I didn't even let anyone know I was on the scale. I stepped off, then back on, hoping I had forgotten to take off some article of clothing that maybe added 10, or 40, pounds.

This was unbelievable! It was a whole new level of discomfort, frustration and humiliation. How did I get HERE? I knew it wasn't going to be good, but I had no idea it was this bad.

The hard part is, it was less about the number on the scale than about what it meant to be that heavy. It meant that I wasn't going to be able to teach my son how to play baseball or basketball. I wouldn't be able to run and play with him. This was crushing to me. My choices had led me to a place that could potentially prevent my son from experiencing all that I had as a child. Playing sports is not the be-all and end-all status for a kid. I know that.

Chapter 1: Wake Up Call

But it was so much a part of my childhood; I had dreamed of having a son that I could play catch with, shoot baskets with and show him how to throw a football. I wanted to coach his teams and be an example, not only for him, but for his friends, too. Now, I felt so far from that, it was hard to fathom.

Maybe you have experienced something similar?

Since you are reading this book, you may have experienced a moment like I did—a time when you realize your vision for your life is not syncing up with the reality of what you are facing. Whether it is because of a scale, or the way your clothes fit, a bad job, broken relationship or something else, most of us have a moment when we come to the realization that we are far from what we want.

If this is you, I have good news for you. First, you are loved and enough, just as you are today. I mean that sincerely. (You may need to go back and read that again.) Second, you are not alone. Third, you can do something about whatever it is you are facing. It may not look "perfect" or "the way it's supposed to be," but you can do something.

The realization of where I was and how far I had drifted from what I really wanted was shocking. I had tried hard in the past to make the changes necessary to be who I wanted to be, but I couldn't follow through. The reason was I never had a real purpose or "why" to make a significant, lasting change. But now, I had one—my son!

That day I decided to make a change. I decided that I wasn't going to give up on myself, my wife or my son. I was going to start making better choices THAT DAY and begin moving towards my goals. I decided I was going to start with small steps instead of trying to make a drastic change again.

I started a new approach.

Instead of looking in the mirror and thinking, "You need to lose 50 pounds, fatty," which is what I would typically do (self-defeating talk is NEVER helpful, by the way), I took a different approach. I decided I was going to focus on my actions, make small incremental changes and lose 10 pounds at a time, instead of 50 all at once.

Actually, my first goal was just to NOT weigh 290. So, 289 it was.

I started by making small changes. I didn't wait until I got back to my house or until the holidays were over. I started moving that day. I did a short workout at my in-law's house and changed how I ate for the remainder of the trip. Eating one plate of food instead of repeats and cutting out the sweets.

Once I got back home, I had to make some changes in my daily routine that would allow for small changes that were sustainable. Although they weren't going to create the sexy "BIG" weight loss that our culture craves, it allowed me to sustain the habits over the

Chapter 1: Wake Up Call

long term. I believed that consistency of effort, both for food and for exercise, was more important than intensity.

At that time, I was a traveling sales rep. My work day would start around 7:30 a.m., by driving to a car dealership to meet with their finance team to help them sell more cars. Since they were working on selling cars and were busy, one of the easiest ways to get their attention was to bring food in for them. I constantly took food into car dealerships to feed the staff. I had a budget for lunches or breakfasts, but also had to make the dollars spread so I could visit more stores. I generally chose cheap food like pizza and donuts, because it was easy and did the job. When you take food like that into the dealership, it's hard not to eat it. It's also hard to lose weight when you are eating pizza multiple times per week. When you don't have a specific goal, allowing yourself "one little snack" like a donut doesn't seem like a big deal. But, when you add that up over time, it becomes a big problem. Have you ever been there?

So, the first steps in my approach were simple. I decided that I wasn't going to eat the food that I took into the dealerships. I was going to drink at least half my body weight in ounces of water, and I would walk two miles a couple of days per week.

It wasn't extraordinarily difficult, but in hindsight, it was extremely effective. I was able to start making progress with small steps, expecting that over time I would build upon the success I was having. I knew at some point, I would have to increase intensity of nutrition and exercise to get to a big weight loss goal, but I wanted to stay consistent. Focusing on taking the right actions was foundational for my success.

Starting out, I had some quick success and within a couple weeks, I hit the first goal! 289! Boom! I was PUMPED! Celebrating success is huge in achieving goals. The hard part is choosing to celebrate in a way that doesn't undermine your big goals. Often, we think that if we hit a weight loss goal, then we can eat (insert unhealthy food choice here). While there is a time to celebrate with eating a meal or something you love that may not be there healthiest choice, now was not the time for me. I was seeing progress and now was the time to keep it going!

So, I set a new goal–279 pounds.

At this point, I decided I would keep all the new habits I had, but I committed to not eating any fast food, except from Subway. The other problem with being on the road all day, every day, is that even if you pack your meals most days, you might not feel like eating them. This was typical of me at this point. As I got better, I chose to eat out less, but at the beginning, I still loved McDonald's or having a Gargantuan Sandwich from Jimmy John's. (That sandwich with chips and a drink is around 1,500 calories!) So, I chose Subway as my only fast food, and would eat a double chicken breast 6" sandwich with cheese, veggies and mustard as the only condiment. I still ate chips, but mostly baked Lays.

Chapter 1: Wake Up Call

I also increased some of my exercise intensity. As I was able to complete my walks faster, I added ankle weights to challenge myself.

It took me between 5-6 weeks and, BOOM, I hit my next goal of 279 pounds! I was rolling! I felt so much better, but still didn't feel like I was depriving myself. I also wasn't focused on being perfect. I was focusing on being better. Now, it was time to celebrate a little and keep the train rolling!

What was the next goal? You guessed it—269.

On paper, this seems easy, but it wasn't. It took effort, planning and support. Throughout this time, Theresa was working to lose some baby weight from her pregnancy with Riley. It was extremely important to have her join me, to be supportive and to keep me on track. One of the next big changes we made was to how we were eating at home. Theresa made dinner EVERY NIGHT! We ate together around 5:30 p.m. This was a change. When we first got married, we used recipes that had been given to us from family and friends. Let's just say that they were not the best choices in food. They were hearty meals that were designed to feed five–ten people. Well, when you are feeding two and there is enough for more than five, it tends to get eaten. Around the time of my next goal, Theresa made some big changes to how we were eating at home. She got rid of some of the old recipes, found new ones, and changed the serving sizes to fit our family's needs. This, along with increasing exercise intensity and keeping all my new habits, led me to achieve my next goal–269 pounds!

Next, I stopped eating out almost completely, and started carrying all of my meals with me every day. Combined with more exercise, and maintaining my new habits, it was only another five-six weeks until I hit 259.

More small changes led to 249.

One step at a time, small changes each time and consistent effort led me to make small goals that added up BIG TIME.

Before my birthday on July 2nd, I was down 50 pounds!

50 pounds of weight lost in six months!!!

What once felt impossible, was now ACCOMPLISHED! It was amazing to see the progress build over time.

The biggest key was that I had a purpose. I had a WHY—being a great dad to my son—which led me to the WHAT and HOW.

Often, we think we need to have the whole plan laid out before us in order to make a change, but really, the key is to know the results you want and to start taking action towards those results. I didn't plan out each phase of the journey. I didn't know in advance what it would take to hit the goal, but I knew it would take action.

Chapter 1: Wake Up Call

Have you ever felt like you don't know what to do to hit a goal?

Have you felt defeated because everything is not perfectly laid out?

You don't have to see the whole staircase to have success. You just have to take the first step. Seriously, as corny as that may sound, it is the absolute truth!

Because I continued to build upon my success, I was fired up to continue to make MORE progress. I wasn't satisfied with the 50 pounds; I wanted to go beyond that now. Once I got down around the 240-range, I decided I wanted to kick it up a notch and begin competing in bodybuilding competitions again.

Around August of 2006, I joined a gym and started training as a natural bodybuilder. It was something that I had done previously, having won the 2001 NANBF Mr. Natural Illinois Novice Division in 2001.

Between 2007 and 2009, I maintained a bodyweight that was around 220-230 pounds, roughly 70-80 pounds lighter than I had been for the previous three years! I was working out five-six days per week, striving to earn my natural pro card to compete as a professional.

As challenging as the weight loss journey was, this was difficult in its own way. The challenge of trying to add lean muscle without gaining weight or while losing weight isn't an easy task.

I competed in 2009 and was disappointed to place 6th.

So, I tried again the following year, competing in a very tough competition in Dekalb, Illinois, called the OCB Midwest States Bodybuilding Show. In the lead-up to the competition, I had lost so much weight, that I weighed in at 194 pounds the day before the competition. That meant that I had lost 100 pounds since I started this journey!

While losing 100 pounds was never my goal, it was a significant achievement. It was a point that I won't forget because I had dramatically changed my life. I was able to be the dad that I wanted to be. In June 2010, we welcomed our second son, Cooper, and not long after Colton! Being healthy, with lots of energy was now more important than ever. I now had two boys, and I was coaching Riley's baseball team, which was probably my favorite thing to do. The energy I achieved because I prioritized my health led to dramatic changes in my life and the lives of our kids, their friends and more.

Today, I continue to maintain a weight around 230 pounds, which has been my norm for a few years. I PRIORITIZE my health, not just for myself, but to be there for my wife and kids. I now have three boys who require a lot of energy, so it is important for me to make sure I stay physically healthy in order to give them my best.

Throughout the process of weight loss and transformation, something else happened. I got a feeling that what I was doing,

Chapter 1: Wake Up Call

working in corporate America, wasn't for me. After my last bodybuilding competition in November of 2010, I decided I was done competing in bodybuilding. It was tough on me and very tough on my family. Restrictive eating can make you crabby, and I was done with that. I was looking for a new avenue to success. So, in July of 2011, I started studying to make a return to personal training, which I had done in 2001 after my first bodybuilding competition. I decided to take the Certified Strength and Conditioning Specialist (CSCS) through the NSCA. Because I was a Marketing major, I lacked the anatomy and physiology background most have when they take this exam. I also had three kids by this time (ALL boys!), and I was working for Merck in pharmaceutical sales. I studied in the morning before work, at lunch and then at night after the kids had gone to bed. It felt like it took forever to get prepared for this exam. But on December 12, 2013, I passed my CSCS exam! It was a long process, but it was worth it! I began training clients in a 300 sq. ft. space in my basement before and after work. The space was small, my equipment was limited, but it was a huge learning experience for me and a great opportunity to grow as a trainer. I did this routine for a little over a year until it became clear that I could not continue the pace I was at.

Throughout this time, we talked to many friends and family about what we were thinking and how we wanted to move forward. I could continue to work for Merck, probably for a long time, since I made great money with great benefits. The other option was that I could take a massive risk, leave it all and chase the dream. We met with people, prayed, gathered information, had strategy sessions, and prayed some more. Theresa and I were fortunate to meet David Black, a physical therapist who liked the philosophy of what we wanted to do. He decided he wanted to partner with us in this venture. The thing about Dave is that he is an action taker, and he pushed us to start making real significant steps toward opening the doors.

We sat through branding and naming sessions, picking and choosing what was going to be our name, logo, brand. After numerous sessions sifting through tons of choices, we narrowed our choices down.

On April 1, 2015, Movement Fitness, LLC was born on paper. We had a name and a logo. Now we needed a space. We negotiated for months at a couple of different properties until we found one that we loved. It was close to our house, which was super convenient, but it was also out of our price range. The second property, while less than ideal, was a good space, about the same size, but would require more work to prepare. The location also wasn't great. While we were on our third round of negotiations on the second place, the first landlord called back and asked what it would take to get us in the space. We said he needed to match the offer we made on the other location, which was significantly less. He accepted, and we had a home.

Chapter 1: Wake Up Call

My next step was to quit my job in corporate America. It was a tough decision. None of this was truly "REAL" until I left my job. I believe that the way you do one thing is the way you do everything, and even though I didn't love that job, I gave it my best effort. So much so that two months before I quit, I was on a trip in Cancun, Mexico, with the top one percent in the company. I had earned the Vice President's Award for 2014. They took us on a week-long vacation filled with relaxation, fun, and a lot of connecting with the higher-ups in the company. On this trip, I could have taken the opportunity to switch jobs, move on to a new position and stayed with the company. Seriously, it was tough to be there and know what was coming. But both Theresa and I knew what the right thing to do was. We knew that it was time, and if we didn't do it now, the likelihood that we would do it before our kids were grown was slim. So, on my birthday, July 2, 2015, I called my boss and put in my two-weeks' notice. That was it. Movement Fitness was officially going to happen.

We are now in year three of Movement Fitness, and I could not be more grateful for it! It is a coaching-based facility that specializes in custom training for adults and athletic performance training for young athletes. I have the privilege of working with people to help them achieve their physical goals and to help them set their sights higher in order to reach their fullest potential.

I am writing this book because I have personally experienced disappointment and know what it feels like to not be my best. But I also know what it is like to live a disciplined and determined life that makes an impact on those around me. The work we do at Movement Fitness has helped over a thousand people who have struggled to achieve a goal, but now have the tools to live their best life yet! I understand that you have your own struggles in life. Whether it is a struggle with weight, self-confidence, job satisfaction, financial debt, family life, I believe this book will provide you with the motivation AND the tools to help you begin moving towards your goals TODAY!

First, I want to help you understand a couple of things:

1. You are enough, right now. I believe that you have been created and are loved more than you will ever know. You don't have to change for other people or to meet someone else's expectations.

2. You are capable of more! Knowing you are enough and reaching your full potential are two different things. I want to encourage you to strive to become the BEST version of yourself every single day. If you do, you will find a life that, while challenging, will bring fulfillment and contentment like you have never known before.

Whatever made you pick up this book, know that I pray it will help you to become your best version of yourself.

The saying, "Be Great Today," is specific and purposeful. If you have ever heard someone say, "Have a great day" or "Make it a great day," you know it is because they wish you well.

Chapter 1: Wake Up Call

In reality, you can't always HAVE a great day, as I mentioned at the beginning of this book. Seriously, have you ever had a bad day? I have. On the other hand, we can't always MAKE something happen. We can't control the way other people think, for example.

But in ALL things, we can choose to BE great. We can choose to lift ourselves and others up in tough times, to be a lighthouse for those that need a path, while also choosing greatness in everyday tasks. This is all done through intentional attitude and actions.

I hope this book inspires you to be more and to reach your fullest potential every day. Along with that, I want it to give you specific action items to help you start making progress now. Knowledge without action is useless, so we want you to start taking steps to achieve your goals!

As you turn the page to begin, make sure you are ready to dive in deep. Be prepared to dig into the core of who you are, get motivated, and start taking action on the chapters and specific items outlined here. Know that today you are enough, you are capable, and you can choose to Be Great Today!

Chapter 2

Wake Up on Purpose

IMAGINE THAT YOUR ALARM clock just went off! You JUMP out of bed and the energy is FLOWING! You WOKE UP ON PURPOSE! You know EXACTLY what you are going to do today. You have specific tasks you are going to achieve, and you know where you are going to go.

You are on a MISSION!

Ever have a day like that?

Was it this morning?

Unfortunately, this is the EXCEPTION, rather than the norm.

Most days, we wake up, hit the snooze button, roll over and wish that the second alarm wouldn't go off. We don't want to have to go to work or school. We want to stay in bed. But we HAVE to get up. We HAVE to go to work in order to pay the bills and keep our jobs. We HAVE to go to school in order to graduate on time.

Chapter 2: Wake Up on Purpose

Most people live their lives on HAVE to.

Most of us lack true purpose.

We know WHAT we have to do, we know WHEN we have to do it, but we don't REALLY know WHY.

Do you know your WHY?

Not the "because I have to pay the bills" or "because my mom said I have to go to school," but the REAL why!

The deep-down, set-your-soul-on-FIRE purpose?

I am talking about the purpose that wakes you up in the morning and drives you to constantly strive to become more. It is the thing that gets you out of bed, even on those cold days where you want to stay curled up in the blankets. It is the purpose that drives you to get up and move forward even after getting knocked down.

Have you ever met someone with purpose?

They have passion and energy. They walk with intentionality. They get to work early and are extremely productive. They have great relationships with the people around them. They are consistent and committed to the things that are important to them.

These people have a reason, a purpose, a WHY! They know, within the core of their being, what THE most important thing is that they have to do today in order to get them to their GOALS.

They know the results they want and take massive action towards achieving those plans. They don't waste time, and their productivity within 24 hours makes you wonder how they accomplish so much. They also tend to have great relationships with their family and friends. From the outside, it seems like everything goes their way, and they never have bumps in the road. In reality, though, they actually have TWICE as many road bumps as you. However, they are persistent and find a way rather than giving up.

Instead of giving up on the last project that was a failure, they pushed through and found a solution that made the project a hit. Instead of allowing an argument with their spouse to derail their relationship, they work through the difficulty to make sure that they maintain a positive marriage.

When was the last time that you were persistent? The last time that you stood up in the face of adversity and did not waiver?

Have you done that recently?

If you did, it felt good, right?

As you think back on that moment, you're filled with pride. You made up your mind that you weren't going to give up. You made a choice that you were going to fight for what was right and do the best you could, no matter what, in order to get the job done.

Today, you have the opportunity to start fresh. Each day is a new chance to do something that has NEVER been done before. You can make a new choice today to start, restart or quit

Chapter 2: Wake Up on Purpose

something that will change your life, forever. You have a choice. Are you ready?

In order to become the person you want to be, you first have to know your WHY.

If you do not have a DEEP purpose, a reason for being, you will struggle to move in a positive direction. You will take one step forward and one step back leading to this perpetual cycle of frustration.

The DEEP why will get you up in the morning! It will help you kick the covers off, fight the urge to stay in bed and get ready to dominate the day.

Think about this. Why is it that every time we go on vacation, we pick the flight that makes us get up at 3 a.m. to make it to the airport on time? I know we want to get to our destination as soon as possible, but why SO early? *It is because we have a purpose.* We have intentionally set this time apart so that we can be together with our family and get away from the fast-paced life we live every day. You know exactly what you have to do. You have a task list of things you need to get accomplished. If you're anything like my family, my superwoman wife gets everything together for our kids, gets herself ready, then leaves me a list of stuff I need to do for myself and what to pack into the car. She has set the playbook for the day so nothing goes wrong. We pack all our clothes and make sure we don't leave a kid behind, Home Alone-style. It is a pretty effective system.

So, let me ask you, why don't you do that during the regular weekday mornings? Why do we hit snooze, roll over and hope the alarm doesn't go off again? Why do we put ourselves in a position where we are running around frantically trying to get out the door, get to work in just enough time to not be late (or sneak in the door where no one will see we're late) or get the kids to school or the bus drop off just in the nick of time? It's because we lack purpose.

When you don't have anything to get up for, then why would you get up any earlier than you have to? If you do not know *why* you are getting up in the morning, you will hit the snooze button. The snooze button serves one purpose, to KILL POTENTIAL. That's its job, and it does it well.

If you do not know your WHY, what your #1 purpose is, then you need to stop and do some self-evaluation.

This is the hard work.

You will have to stop your busy life, reflect on where you are and think about where you want to go. It is not easy. You will have to get quiet and "listen to the whispers," as my mentor, Todd Durkin says. You have to battle through the stuff of everyday life in order to get to your real purpose.

If you are ready to do that, then get out a piece of paper and pencil and start writing this stuff down!

Here are some questions to ask if you do not know what your purpose is:

Chapter 2: Wake Up on Purpose

Part 1:

1. What makes your soul sing?
2. What makes you smile? (people, places, hobbies, projects)
3. What are you doing when you feel most alive?
4. What activities are you doing when you lose track of time?
5. What are you willing to fight for?
6. To whom do you want to be a hero?
7. Who inspires you?
8. What is your biggest regret?
9. What is your dream?
10. When was the last time you took action towards your dream?
11. What could you do right now to start moving towards your goal?
12. How could this year be different from last year?
13. If you were living your best life, what would it look like?
    a. in one Week
    b. in one Month
    c. in one Year
    d. in one Decade

Part 2:

1. What season of life are you in?

    a. *Do you have young kids?*

    b. *Are you an empty-nester?*

    c. *Are you single?*

    d. *Are you looking for personal development?*

    e. *Do you need to make money?*

2. *Is your job to be a provider for your family?*

    a. *Financially*

    b. *Emotionally*

    c. *Spiritually*

3. *What are the things you must do right now?*

4. *In spite of all the things you must do, what can you start doing right now to move towards your goals?*

5. *Imagine yourself at 90 years old, reflecting back on your life—of all the things you have done, what are you most grateful for?*

Take some time to dig into these questions.

Seriously, over the next week, schedule some time in your calendar when you are going to go through these questions. Then go over them again.

Part 1 of the questions is digging into your why, your purpose. Everyone has one, if you are willing to dig for it. For some it may come easily. You read the first line, and it immediately popped into your head. For others, it won't be so easy. It will take time and effort to dig in, but if you dedicate the time to finding your purpose, then you can start making significant strides today! Once you start to pinpoint this PURPOSE, it will start to orient your life!

The second part is to bring awareness to where you are currently in life. It is critical to be self-aware of your age and stage of life.

For some, you will get discouraged by Question 2 in this section. I know it was a barrier for me when I was working in my corporate job and was the primary breadwinner, with a wife, three kids, a mortgage and more. For a long time, that was a damper on my dream of opening a training facility. Many times, I thought that there was no way it was going to happen. "How am I ever going to be able to quit this job?" But Question 3 was what started getting me moving towards my goal. What could I do RIGHT NOW, despite all that is going on in my life? I started to study for certifications, then I started training people at my home, their home or the gym. It wasn't perfect. It was difficult. But it allowed me to start moving in the direction of my goals. This is where you have to be driven by your purpose. Every scenario is different but having a purpose will keep you from getting discouraged and prevent you from retreating when the odds look like they are stacked against you.

The last question is probably the most difficult. Try to imagine yourself getting old and think back to what would have been truly important. What is the legacy you want to leave? Whatever it is, you can start today to set your sights on a bigger purpose You can prevent little things from taking you off track and distracting you. Your legacy, what you want to leave behind, will orient you in a direction that will provide clarity.

Your purpose or WHY may change over time, but what shouldn't change is the desire to push to become the best version of yourself.

Have you ever thought about being in command of your day and what that would look like?

What is the first thing you are going to work on in the morning?

What time will you go to bed?

When will you eat?

What is the PRIORITY, the one thing that has to get done?

Do you know?

Most of us go through life without a specific purpose, and that overflows into our days. We end up living this Groundhog's Day kind of life that seems to just repeat. We get tired of the same job, same house, same cars, running the kids to and from events, day after day. We live by reacting to the world around us.

What if, instead, you took control of your life, knew your purpose and let that dictate your days? What freedom would that provide? What joy would that give you, even in the face of the toughest challenges in life? It would create a completely different outcome.

Having that kind of purpose though, will require that you take responsibility for everything that happens to you. The good, the bad, the unfair—all of it. It means that you will have to take control so that you can choose to be great in all scenarios.

Recap:

Did you dig into the questions outlined in Chapter 1?

_____

If so, write your purpose here:

_____

_____

_____

_____

What do you value most in life?

_____

_____

_____

_____

Based on this purpose, what are the three-five actions you need to start taking today?

_____

_____

_____

_____

_____

Who/Where do you want to be:

_____

_____

in one week- _____

in one month- _____

in one year- _____

in one decade- _____

Chapter 3

Take Responsibility and Choose to Be Great

"The price of greatness is responsibility."
—Winston Churchill

BEFORE YOU DO ANYTHING else, right now, you are going to take responsibility for YOUR life.

I believe you were created for a purpose, and you are capable of amazing things. However, we are often reactive instead of proactive with our own lives. We wait for life to come to us instead of the other way around. Rather than being intentional with our attitude and our actions, we wait. We are haphazard in our approach which leads us to placing blame on others for the things that are going wrong in our lives. By placing blame on others, we give someone or something else the power to influence and direct your life.

Chapter 3: Take Responsibility and Choose to Be Great

You're allowing another person to "ruin your day" or "make you do something," because of something they said or did. Don't give away your power. Do not allow someone else to be in control of your life.

Jocko Willink, former Navy Seal and author of **Extreme Ownership: How U.S. Navy SEALs Lead and Win**, writes specifically about how taking responsibility for EVERYTHING in your life can have a significant impact on the quality of your life, whether you are in the military, the boardroom or home. He says, "Implementing extreme ownership requires checking your ego and operating with a high degree of humility. Admitting mistakes, taking ownership, and developing a plan to overcome challenges are integral to any successful team."

Taking ownership, being humble, admitting mistakes, and developing a plan—those are the attitudes and actions necessary to take responsibility for your life.

Here is the hard part of taking responsibility of everything in life. We need to be willing to take the bad with the good. We want to be in control—until something goes wrong. Then, we want to pass blame. We look for excuses as to why something happened, rather than taking responsibility for our lives. We accept excuses and neglect to make the changes necessary to correct the path that we are on. Taking responsibility for our lives requires us to look at ourselves mentally, physically, emotionally and spiritually in order to understand where we currently are, and then to begin to make the corrections necessary to get back on the right path.

If you do this, it will mean that you are in more control of what happens to you. You start to live a PROACTIVE life rather than a REACTIVE life. Even when life seems to start happening *TO* you, you can step back, evaluate and start to correct the path you are on.

Bad things are going to happen, no doubt about it. A loved one gets sick, we lose our job, or we get in a car accident. That's all bad, right? Maybe. If we are living a purposeless life, then, yes, it is. You think either God, the Universe or the devil is conspiring against you. But, if we are intentional with our attitude, this is a greater opportunity. It's a chance to realize that nothing happens *TO* us, it happens *FOR* us. These moments allow us to begin to choose to BE great.

If someone gets sick, it becomes an opportunity to deepen a relationship or faith. It provides the priority to tell someone that you love them, to be there to support them or give them comfort in a time of need. That's choosing to BE great.

If you lose your job, maybe it's a chance to finally go do the thing you have been passionate about but were too afraid to take the risk to begin your new career.

I once was laid off from a job because they shut down an entire division of the company. This was a huge event in our lives. I was

Chapter 3: Take Responsibility and Choose to Be Great

27 and had two kids at the time—this was a problem. In reality, it turned out to be a massive blessing because I had an interview the following week and received a job offer for a new company. Because I was laid off, I got paid DOUBLE my salary for six months. It was a huge catalyst for us to get out of debt at that time! Remember, everything is happening *for* you, if you are open to it. Regardless of your circumstances, be intentional and continue to work and move forward. That's choosing to BE great.

Taking responsibility for your life will give you a freedom that you have never had before. It will begin to make you think with intentionality, which will increase your ability to communicate with your spouse, family and friends. It will organize your days, so you know what you are going to do first thing in the morning. It will give you a purpose and a vision that is clear and specific. If you know what you purpose is, then you can start taking responsibility by organizing your days and weeks around the important things in your life.

If you say your family is the most important thing in your life, do they occupy the most time on your calendar? Do they get appropriate amount of time with you to continue to develop and deepen the relationship?

If your spouse is the most important person in your life, are you taking responsibility for the state of your marriage or relationship? Really? Are you planning date nights, setting aside trips for just the two of you or just making sure to create quality time and moments with them?

If you say your faith is important to you, is that exemplified in the way you talk to people and how you treat them? Do you pray or meditate first thing in the morning? Do you live your life in such a way that it is abundantly clear that you are a believer?

When you state your purpose and list the important people or things in your life, then you can start to take responsibility by simply looking at your calendar and seeing if what you say is true.

All of us need help! No one can do this on their own. You need to find someone to hold you accountable for the things you say and do.

Recap:

Fill in the blanks:

By placing _____ on others, we give someone or something else the _____ to influence and direct your life.

Answer these questions:

What area of your life do you need to start taking responsibility for today?

_____

Chapter 3: Take Responsibility and Choose to Be Great

_____

Your Faith?

_____

Your Marriage/Relationship?

_____

Your Family?

_____

Your Job?

_____

Your Weight/Body?

_____

How can you start taking responsibility for your actions today?

_____

_____

Have you ever had a "bad" thing happen to you that turned out to be great?

_____

_____

_____

Chapter 4

Be Specific

"Specificity is the key to achievement."
—Ed Mylett

IN JANUARY 2006, I flew to Florida to pick up Theresa and move her back to Illinois. We met her dad and uncle in Orlando, packed up everything out of her apartment and then began the 24-hour, 1,000-mile journey. When we left, we had one goal—bring her back to Illinois. It was simple. We set a specific destination as our target. We set the GPS and followed the route all the way back home. It wasn't rocket science. We knew exactly where we were going. We had a goal and set up the process to get us home. We knew exactly how long it would take, where we were going to stop and how much gas we were going to need.

Chapter 4: Be Specific

For too many of us, we don't have goals in life and we certainly don't have a process for how to achieve them. We have thoughts like:

I want to be happy.

I want to be in shape.

I want to be healthy.

I want a better job.

Here's the truth about statements like those above. They are filled with hope, but no direction. They require no strategy, because they have no destination. What does, "I want to be happy" mean, anyway? Are you frustrated with yourself, your life conditions, your attitude, your finances, your lack of faith? How exactly do you plan on being happy?

What about, for example, "I want to be in shape." What exactly is "in shape" for you? Is it a weight goal, body composition change or do you want to be able to run a marathon? Those are all VERY different things.

It is so important if you are going to reach a physical goal that you are specific. When I talked earlier about losing weight, I broke down my journey into small, 10-pound increments, but the first big goal was to lose 50 pounds There was no doubt. I established the systems and processes that I needed so that I would hit those goals. After that, when I went into bodybuilding, I had a goal—to earn my professional card. I knew exactly where I needed to be in order to achieve that goal. I knew that I would have to get up at 5 a.m. to eat. I would have to train 7-10 times per week between strength and cardio workouts, and I would need to get my sleep to recover.

Your brain and your accountability partner have a hard time holding you to, "I want to be in better shape." But they sure can hold you to 10 percent bodyfat by March 1st, or 200 pounds by (insert date). Along the way, if you have the right strategy, they can hold you accountable to the process and system you set up to hit your goals.

Are you eating according to the goals you set?

Are you getting in to the gym enough times per week?

Do you have a strategy to help you not overeat?

You cannot simply hope you are going to get to your goals.

Hope is not a strategy.

Read that again.

Hope is not a strategy.

It begs, wishes and wants for things to come true, but doesn't require anything of you other than the mental space. This is why you have failed previously. You set the intention to do something good, but you didn't act on it. It's like getting in a car and driving,

Chapter 4: Be Specific

hoping you are going to get somewhere, but you don't know where you are going. This causes massive frustration and is self-defeating.

If you have a purpose in life and take full responsibility for your actions, you need to write down your specific goals to create a map. Your goals will give you a destination, from which you can start marking out your path. Before you can start designing the route, you have to know the destination.

We struggle with this because we live in a fast-paced, microwave society. We want everything done now. We have a general idea of a goal, but it's too broad. By being general and not specific, we allow ourselves to become self-defeating. This is a protective strategy we take in order to not achieve our full potential, because we are afraid. If you don't have a specific goal, then you don't have anything that people can hold you accountable to. This is a recipe for disaster. You want to go somewhere, but you don't want to have anyone hold you to your word. Setting a goal of losing 50 pounds is a BIG deal. It means that you are going to have to put in time and effort, develop a plan and follow it and have people hold you accountable to that goal. But if you say things like, "I just want to be healthy," that has no specificity, and no one will be able to hold you accountable. Good luck trying to get where you want to go.

Rather than that, take the time to evaluate your life.

Really.

Where are you today?

Where do you want to go?

What are your dreams?

Now, the difficult part is, you will have to do this for multiple areas of your life.

Faith

Marriage/Relationships

Being a Parent

Weight/Health

Career/Job

Friendships

Future

etc.

Any area of life that you give time and effort to needs a road map. This seems like a daunting task, but this will give you freedom. Jocko Willinck uses the phrase, "Discipline equals Freedom." IF you are disciplined enough to write down VERY specific goals, it will create purpose, direction and narrow your focus.

I struggle with this significantly. I am afraid to say no to people. I don't want to disappoint others, but I also have a desire to be wanted. If I don't do it, someone else will and that would mean I'm not as important or as good as someone else. It's a crappy way

Chapter 4: Be Specific

to think. Instead, let's narrow the scope of our focus, be REALLY, insanely great at what we were meant to do and leave the rest to others.

Create the structure in your life and in your days that will allow you to be the best at what you were meant to do. Give up the need to feel important and give up the ambiguity of broad goals.

In order to go one step beyond being specific, you are going to write down your goals as if they have already happened. This goes way beyond hope and starts tapping into faith—faith in GOD, faith in yourself, faith in the people around you. Once you move away from hope as a strategy for goal achievement and into the realm of faith, things will start happening to you at a rapid pace. Seriously. Ed Mylett talks about this all the time. He says, "Our subconscious mind will work to prove you right." Meaning, if you believe that something positive or negative is going to happen, your brain will make it so. Honestly. When was the last time you had a negative thought and then something positive happened? Rarely. If you think that people are out to get you or that nobody cares about you, then for the most part, that will come true. Someone will cut you off in traffic and you will be all pissed off saying, "I knew it, the whole world is out to get me."

Shift that mindset to something positive instead. Believing that there is good out there and that GOD or other people want to help make you successful. If you take that mindset, then your whole outlook on life will change.

As you write your goals, allow your subconscious mind to work FOR you. Get rid of the hope. Get rid of the negative, self-defeating thoughts and start acting as if it has already happened. Start having faith that the things you want to happen will come true. I promise it will shift everything for you.

Be honest with yourself, be specific about what you want, and be disciplined enough to write down what you want to happen, as if they already have.

To help you out, here are my goals:

1. I have a faith in God, through his son, Jesus, that is so strong and lived out in my daily life that five people have come to know Jesus this year.
2. I have a thriving marriage with my wife. I create four hours per week that is dedicated to us, intentional time, quality time, through home and outside date nights.
3. I am a patient and loving father, helping my kids grow individually and as a group of three. I spend one hour per week with each of my sons alone, in order to give them the time they need as individuals.
4. We have four nights per week at home for dinner.
5. I am the owner of a fitness company worth $10 million that specializes in athletic performance training, personal training and development, nutrition, and self-improvement. We have a state-of-the-art facility

that provides the highest quality coaching, the best in equipment, and is the destination site for athletes and adults looking to reach their peak performance.

6. I am a sought-after authority on Speed Development for Athletic Performance.
7. I am the author of New York Times bestsellers on how to create your best life, leadership and faith.
8. I am a sought-after speaker that influences 5,000 people annually through 50 paid speaking appointments.
9. I keep myself in peak physical condition at 10 percent body fat
10. I give away $1 million annually to charities in my community, nationally and around the world.
11. I write 1000 words or more every day.
12. I listen to one uplifting or self-improvement podcast every day.
13. I read at least one book per month on athletic performance (or program/certification).
14. I read at least one book per month on leadership, self-development or faith.
15. I am a partner with a major apparel company.

What were your goals for the previous year?

Did you achieve them?

What are your top three-five goals for this year?

For your:

Faith

Marriage/Relationships

Parenting

Weight/Health

Career/Job

Friendships

Future

How much money do you want to make?

_____

_____

Why do you want to make that much?

_____

_____

What specifically do you want to accomplish with your body this year?

_____

How are you going to grow in your career?

Chapter 4: Be Specific

_____

_____

_____

How can you develop and demonstrate your faith to others?

_____

_____

_____

How can you be a better husband, wife, partner this year?

_____

_____

_____

What other specific goals do you want to achieve?

_____

_____

_____

What systems are you going to put in place to help you achieve these goals?

_____

Chapter 5

GO!

"Act as if it were impossible to fail."
—DOROTHEA BRANDE

I RECENTLY SET AN intention to speak at a church. It is something that I have wanted to do for a while, but because I didn't do anything with it, it really was a wish, not a goal. So, I set the intention and wrote it as a specific goal. As I was starting to write it in this book in the previous chapter, I realized that I should reach out to my pastor and let him know. I texted him to let him know my intention and why I wanted to speak. He responded back with a text that said, "Great, I love it."

Um, I was hoping for a little more excitement, but I thought, "Okay, cool. At least he knows my intention."

Chapter 5: Go!

Then about five minutes later, he sends me another text and says, "Actually, we are talking about health and how it impacts our faith for a teaching series just after the new year. I would love to talk to you about this." The next day we had lunch. He invited me to be a part of a Faith and Health teaching in three weeks and then asked if I would teach a two-hour seminar on Faith and Fitness later that month!

BOOM!

Are you kidding me?

See, I believe that GOD works things out. I also believe that if you don't take the first step, there is no way that would have happened. Here is the other thing I know; if you set your intentions, your brain will start to work to make it happen. For this specific goal, I set the intention and then took ACTION!

Tony Robbins has a saying that goes like this, "Lacking resources is never the problem, lacking resourcefulness is the problem." When I set the intention, wrote my goal, I also DID something to make it come true. We get wrapped up in this idea that we don't have what it takes to achieve our goals. It's a load of garbage. Really. You may not have the money for the business you want to open today, but if you show enough value to enough people, you will. You might not have all the "right" equipment or the "perfect" weight loss plan to begin getting in shape, but if you do something, the plan begins to develop and evolve. You don't have to see the entire staircase to get to the top. You just have to take the first step.

Seriously, that may sound cliché, but it's true. If you are waiting for the perfect time to do something new or make a change, the time is NOW! Start by writing out a list of goals and intentions and then start moving towards them!

Take one step.

Make the phone call.

Create the content.

Skip the carbs.

Say "I'm sorry."

Schedule the date night.

Ask the favor.

Do THE Thing!

I believe this. If you take action today, something good will happen for you. Whether you believe in GOD or not, I think that is true. Setting your intention sets your mind. Thinking and writing is SO good, but action is what is going to make it happen. Don't get caught up in what other people think. Don't fear rejection or get bogged down in trying to please others.

Be You. Authentically You. If you are well-intentioned and looking to provide value to others, even when you make mistakes, people will understand. Those that matter, don't mind, and those that mind, don't matter.

Now, when you look at your list of goals, you will have short-, medium- and long-term goals. I don't expect to have a $10 million facility tomorrow. That is a long-term goal for me. I do want to keep that goal in the forefront of my mind, though, because it influences everything that I do with my business. It influences the choices that I make, the content I create and the conversations I'm having. It is important for me to communicate WHY I want this facility. How do I prepare myself and others for that reality? I am going to start acting like that now, so that when we get there, we know who we are and are true to ourselves.

Because of my relationship with my pastor, I knew speaking at a church could be a short-term goal. I didn't know it would happen THAT fast, but I knew it could happen. Setting intentional time with my wife is an actionable, specific goal for me. It's something that can be done in the short term and will make our marriage stronger.

Take the time to set your intentions and be specific with your goals—but then get off your butt and start making them happen. Act specifically.

If this is an area of struggle, you may need to get a calendar or planner to write out what you want to achieve. Be specific and think big. Our issues stem not from thinking too big, but from thinking too small. Go BIG. Shoot for the moon. Seriously.

You also will need an accountability coach or partner to push you forward. It's not just about being active for the sake of movement, it's about taking action that is going to help you get closer to your goals. John Ruskin once said, *"What we think or what we know or what we believe is, in the end, of little consequence. The only consequence is what we do."*

Be an action taker.

Recap:

Have you written down your goals?

_____

If no, Why not?

_____

If yes, are they specific?

_____

_____

What are three-five things you could do RIGHT NOW to help you achieve your goals?

_____

_____

_____

Chapter 5: Go!

Who do you need to reach out to help you achieve your goals?

_____

_____

_____

Do you have a planner or notebook that can help you stay organized?

_____

_____

Do you write in it weekly?

_____

Daily?

_____

What do you need to do to be more intentional with your goals and actions?

_____

_____

_____

_____

Chapter 6

Getting Accountability

> *"If you want to go fast, go alone.
> If you want to go far, go together."*
> —African Proverb

WE ALL NEED ACCOUNTABILITY. From the "strongest" person you know to the "weakest," we all need someone to keep us accountable for the things we've said are the most important.

The problem most of us face is that we want to go fast. We live in a "microwave" society that says we need to do everything faster. The problem is, very few things that happen fast, last. We look for the new fad in weight loss, the way-to-make-a-quick buck scheme or the best hack to achieve our next goal. Unfortunately, there is no such thing as a shortcut or hack for something that is worthwhile or lasting.

Chapter 6: Getting Accountability

The hard part is, when we get motivated, we want to capitalize on that motivation quickly in order to build momentum. This drives us to do the easiest thing to create a positive change or we go back to the thing that helped us last time. For example, if you are starting your weight loss again and you start using what worked last time, it probably won't last, because if you have to start over again, then last time didn't really work. It may have created a short-term change, but short-term changes aren't exactly the goal.

What we really need is accountability.

Ugh. The dreaded word. Most of us despise accountability, because it means we have to own up to what we said we were going to do. This is the single best way to stay on track, but it is also the most uncomfortable. It means that you have to tell someone what you are doing consistently to make sure it will get you to where you want to go.

When I was bodybuilding, I hired a coach to provide me with a plan to get me in the best shape possible and to hold me accountable. The plan that he created was good, but it wasn't rocket science. It was a straightforward bodybuilding plan with typical training sessions. The most important part was that I had to check in with him two times per week to let him know how I was doing so he could figure out if we needed to make any changes or not. Every Tuesday and Friday, I sent him the information he requested. I did this for 20 weeks. I finished in the absolute best shape of my life. I needed to go far, so I chose to go together with someone.

Being a coach, I am a huge advocate for hiring someone for support and guidance. I think it is the best way to help provide a plan and accountability. When you pay someone, you have more on the line, skin in the game. You are less likely to waste their time or your own when you make a financial investment.

We need to get someone that can give us a pat on the back or a kick in the pants—preferably someone who knows the difference between the two and when to give them. Whether you hire a professional or get a friend to help you, having accountability can be one of the biggest steps you can take in order to achieve significant and sustained success. If you hire a professional, they should be able to walk you through your calendar, help you plan out the important people and things in your life and prioritize accordingly.

If you choose to find an accountability partner, that's great, too. It probably should NOT be your best friend, though. Your friend is probably more sympathetic to your case than you need from an accountability partner. They love you, so they might struggle to keep you on track. They often don't want to call you out because it would be hard on the relationship. Ideally, it should be someone you don't want to disappoint!

Chapter 6: Getting Accountability

Sometimes, we feel uneasy with an accountability partner or they don't know what to ask to keep us on track. So, when you have the perfect someone, you are going to do two things:

1. Pick two check-in days per week
   a) Side note: choosing two days is ideal because it keeps your accountable on BOTH sides of the weekend. For example, Monday and Friday check-ins require that you don't go off the rails over the weekend.
2. Have them ask you the following questions
   a) Are you on track with your goal? Be as specific with your answer as possible. If weight loss is your goal, use a number or pant size.
   b) Did you take the specific action you said you were going to?
   c) What do you need to change/keep doing to stay on track?

Don't overthink it. Be honest with yourself and your partner. Lying to your accountability partner will eventually cause a significant issue. First, you are fooling yourself about where you really are to look good in a moment, and second, your partner will eventually realize you're lying when you aren't making progress. This will lead them to stop asking questions or caring about what's happening in terms of your goals because they will realize that if you don't care enough to be honest, why should they? Answer the questions, and then think about what needs to be corrected and what needs to be continued.

If you can do this on a consistent basis, you will make significant strides towards your goals. The more honest you are, the faster you will start to get there.

Recap:

Do you want to go far or go fast?

___

___

Do you have an accountability partner?

___

___

Do you have a coach?

___

Right now, answer the following questions...

    a) Are you on track with your goal? (Be as specific as possible. If weight loss is your goal, use a number or pant size.)

    b) Did you take the specific action you said you were going to?

    c) What do you need to change/keep doing to stay on track?

Chapter 7

Focus

"Your intention is the result of where you place your attention."
—Unknown

"YOU'RE FIVE-FOOT NOTHING, 100 and nothing and you barely have a speck of athletic ability. And you hung in there with the best college football team in the land for two years. And you're gonna walk out of here with a degree from the University of Notre Dame. In this life you don't have to prove nothing to nobody but yourself. And after what you've gone through, if you haven't done that by now, it ain't gonna never happen. Now go on back." -Fortune to Rudy, Rudy, 1993.

In 1997, getting ready for my senior year, I was ready to quit playing football. Something in my mind wasn't right, and I was ready to be done. My mom encouraged me to keep going because

Chapter 7: Focus

she knew that if I quit, I would regret it the rest of my life. As I was processing my choices, she had me watch Rudy. After watching that, everything changed for me.

I was 6'2", 200 pounds. I had *some* athletic ability. What I had lost was my heart. Football was never my favorite sport. I preferred baseball. But what I loved about football was the preparation. It was the price you had to pay to get ready physically for the season, including the workouts, the conditioning, the studying and everything. I loved all of that. In order to do any of it, though, you had to have the mental fortitude to be prepared to battle. You couldn't spend an entire summer beating your body up if you weren't mentally engaged or prepared for it.

Rudy was a movie that provided me with significant perspective. It is a story of a boy that dreamed of playing football at the University of Notre Dame. Rudy was an underdog. He didn't have the grades or the athletic ability to get into the school, let alone play football. After high school, he worked in the mill where his dad and brothers worked. He was saving up money to go to Notre Dame, but wasn't getting anywhere fast. Everyone laughed off his dream as a stupid, unrealistic goal until one day, his best friend, Pete, was killed in an accident at work. The incident rocked Rudy. He quit the mill after the funeral and took off for Notre Dame, even though everyone thought he was crazy. He couldn't get admitted, so he had to go to St. Mary's to get his grades up so Notre Dame would accept him. Semester after semester, he was rejected, until his last opportunity, when he got in! Now, he just had to try out to make the team. He made the scout team because of his grit. The scout team runs the opponent's plays against the "real team" so they can practice. Essentially, he got the crap kicked out of him week in and week out. He was promised by the Head Coach, Ara Parseghian, to dress for one varsity game during his senior year. The only problem was, Coach Parseghian quit after Rudy's junior year and the new Coach, Dan Devine, didn't have any interest in allowing Rudy to take the place of a valuable player. Throughout this journey, he worked for and befriended a groundskeeper named Fortune. Fortune served as a mentor to Rudy throughout this time. Despite all of Rudy's best efforts and consistent practicing, Coach Devine declined the opportunity for Rudy to dress for his last game. Rudy decides to quit. Fortune gave him the motivational talk listed above to remind him of how far he had come and that he didn't have to prove anything to anyone—not his father, friends or anyone but himself. Fortune talked him into going back, which Rudy did. At the last minute, Coach Devine changed his mind, and allowed Rudy to dress for the game. While Notre Dame was beating Purdue, the crowd started chanting his name so coach would put him in the game. With ten seconds left on the clock, Rudy went into the game. He covered a kickoff that went out of bounds, with no action. He stayed on the field, and this five-foot nothing, 100 and nothing, kid got a sack as time expired! He was carried off the field—the last Notre Dame player to have that honor. This movie, based on a true story, was a deep and uplifting experience for me at that time and still is today.

After watching it, I was ready to attack my senior year! I was able to take that feeling of excitement and turn it into action. I was mentally ready to take action and prepare myself for the summer ahead, which would ultimately lead to success or failure on the field. I had the best training summer of my life, which led to a great senior year for me, including being named to the All-Conference team. Because of that season, I also received an offer to play football at Monmouth College the following fall. To say that movie began a chain of events that changed my life would be an understatement!

Our subconscious brain works to prove us right. Author Joseph Drumheller says, "Whoever you think you are as a person and however you think the world operates will be reflected back to you in the events of your life."

Our thoughts become things. What you put into your brain will eventually come out in some form. If you are feeding yourself with positivity, then positive things will come out. If you are feeding negativity, that will come out.

It is critical that you fill your head with positive things, but also that you are specific with what you want. Not being specific is the easy way out. Lacking specificity exemplifies having a dream or a wish, rather than a goal. For example, writing "I want to be in shape" is way less powerful than writing "I want to have ten percent body fat," or "I want to weigh XXX pounds by XXX date." Those are specific goals that are measurable, achievable, and timebound.

The hard work comes in sitting down, asking yourself some tough questions and really making a specific plan for your life and then being intentional with your days, weeks, month and year. Think through your days. What are your priorities? But also, think about what or who you are allowing to have influence over your life. What do you do with your time and who or what are you giving authority to to influence your life?

Let's explore this.

Your Time

When you wake up in the morning, do you set your intention for the day, week, month and year? Or do you sleep until the last possible minute, hit the snooze button, and then run around with your hair on fire trying to get ready, get the kids out the door for school and still make it to work on time? This is a recipe for disaster. It sets you up to be impatient, angry and to not be the best spouse, partner, father, mother, business owner, or employee possible. Think about it. You're yelling at your kids because you didn't get up in enough time to get you and them ready? You are frustrated because your pants don't fit, but then you run around like crazy in the morning and eat fast food four days a week just to get something in your belly. Does this describe you at all? Do you have an area in the morning that causes you to live with hurry and haste?

Philosopher Dallas Willard said, "You must *ruthlessly* eliminate hurry from your life ..." Ruthless means doing anything necessary to achieve what you want. That is a BIG task. This sounds difficult, but really, it comes down to being intentional with your time. If you are in a hurry 99 percent of the time, it's your fault. You weren't late to work because of the guy in traffic, construction, or the line at McDonald's was backed up. You were late because you didn't prepare or leave yourself enough time. Your kids didn't make you late, you made yourself late by not getting up in time to get dressed and get out the door, **BEFORE** they got up. Instead of living a hurried life, stop, think about what is important and then organize your life accordingly.

I'm not perfect at this at all. When I am not intentional with my time, I wake up later than I want, and ultimately have to sacrifice something at the end of the day. This is not about perfection, but I can tell you, when I am at my best, I am intentional in setting up my week. I know what my top five priorities are and when the important events or appointments will be. I write out what I want to achieve and then set up my week according to those goals. It is a discipline that needs to be cultivated, and if you do this, it will change your whole week. No more getting caught off guard by an appointment you didn't know you had or missing your workouts because of time commitments. This is an intentional habit that will make a significant difference in your life.

Every day may look a little different, but it is important to write down what you want for that day. This, too, is one of those easy-to-skip exercises because it takes time and requires us to put more thought into our lives. Our days won't always go the way you want, but by being intentional, you know your priorities. That helps you make better choices with your time because you know what is truly important. A little bit of time in the morning or at the end of the previous day can have a massive impact on you, your attitude, and how you act towards others. It will take some adjustment, but five-ten minutes in the morning can make a world of difference.

People

I believe that the people in your life are important. People matter. They can be a huge influence on your life and the direction it takes.

A friend of mine, Mike Hickerson, pastor of Mission Church in Ventura, California, once gave me a great way to look at the people in your life. He said we have three levels of friends—an inner, middle and acquaintance circle.

The inner circle is the five (or so) most important and influential people in your life. They are the ones that you trust—the group you go to when you're having a bad day, when you need advice or need a kick in the butt. These five people will have THE GREATEST influence on your life. They are the ones you call when you need ANYTHING! They have your best interest at heart, know who you are and what you stand for and takes those thoughts into account when giving advice or holding you accountable.

Next is your middle circle. These are the people you enjoy hanging out with and spend semi-regular time with. They are the people who lift you up. While they might not be your "core" people, this is a group with whom you enjoy spending time. It is important to remember their value and that they are important, but they also are not the first call you make when you need something. While you may be close, they do not have all the information about you to make the BEST recommendations for you.

Last is your acquaintance circle. This group is filled with people that run in similar circles and have interests that are close to yours in some ways. This group is fun to hang with occasionally, but certainly should not have a ton of influence on your life. Most likely, if these people are influencing, it is not in a positive way. This is the group where we can get caught up on keeping up with the Joneses. They may be a good influence on you, but they certainly don't know enough of the particulars to be a massive influencer in your life.

This is not to look down on anyone, but a way of remembering that there should be key people in your life who have permission to influence your life and then there are others that should not.

So, with that explanation, spend a minute asking yourself these questions:

Who are the people that have the greatest influence on your life?

With whom do you spend the most time?

The people in your life can have a massive influence on who you are and who you become. Your family, friends, acquaintances, co-workers, fellow students and even strangers can have a huge. It is critical that you surround yourself with the right people on a consistent basis in order to maximize your potential. If you don't, then you risk allowing negative talk and thoughts to come into your life. That negativity can destroy your ideas, hopes, dreams and vision.

If someone in your circle is causing significant negativity, you need to stop giving them power over you. In family situations, this can be extremely difficult. We don't get to choose our family, and I pray yours is great. However, we know that family dynamics are less than ideal for many. First off, if you are in an adversarial or abusive relationship of any kind, you need to get out and get help. It's not okay. Find a professional or go somewhere you can be safe and be in a better environment.

If your family scenario isn't detrimental to your immediate health, but not optimal for growth, then you need to limit the amount of input or feedback you allow others to have in your life. If your dad is negative, blaming others for everything, or doesn't support your dreams, maybe you need to limit the conversations you are having with him about your goals, hopes and dreams. You

Chapter 7: Focus

don't have to diminish your goals, it just means that he is not a person you go to for that subject. If your siblings tell you that you're crazy for chasing a big dream, then maybe they don't need to be involved in the conversation. If someone is not speaking life into your dreams, you can still be in relationship with them and love them, but guard yourself so you prevent them from pulling you down.

Your inner circle of people is the most important group of people to you. You need to be vigilant about that group of five. Sometimes you need to reduce the amount of time you spend with people or even remove some people from your life. It's not easy, but if you want to be the best version of yourself, you'll first have to understand that you are whole and loved right now. Those who speak negatively or blame others most likely won't want you to achieve your goals because they didn't achieve theirs. It's not your fault, so don't let them have influence over you.

If you have friends who are negative, lazy or not pursuing the best version of themselves, you need to evaluate those relationships. If you allow them to speak their truth into you, there is a possibility that they will pull you down rather than lift you up.

The same thing goes for co-workers or fellow students. You are surrounded by people at work or school that can impact you by their actions. Make sure that you are intentional with who you allow to get close to you. Negative co-workers can try to drag you down. Don't allow them to. If you are intentional with your attitude and actions, you can influence that negative person as much as they want to influence you. Eventually, they will either tire of your positivity and leave, or they might get curious and start moving in a more positive direction. Don't get into their petty way of thinking by talking down about others, your boss or the company. If you are in a bad situation, seek advice or help from a supervisor or teacher. If that doesn't work, do everything you can to create a cordial but limited relationship with the negative co-worker.

The bottom line is, you must be vigilant about preventing negative people from influencing your life. The old saying is, show me your friends and I'll show you your future. If you are not selective about who you allow into your inner circle, or who your close friends are, you will fall to their level rather than having them rise to yours.

What

In order to get and keep your mind right, the next thing that needs to be guarded are your ears and eyes.

What are you listening to, watching or reading?

You are 100 percent in control of what you allow into your head.

Chapter 7: Focus

We live in a world that is filled with messaging. Everything has a purpose. The shows we watch, the apps we go to, news we read are all fighting for our attention.

Almost all of us are overstimulated. Think about your phone. If you allow notifications on your phone, you would literally spend almost all day responding to the messages that come through the phone. Every notification also tries to get our attention.

Consequently, every headline has to be powerful, whether it's true or not, just to get you to click on it. Would you click on the link that says, "Sunshine in the forecast for the next few days?" No. They gave you the information you needed—it's going to be sunny. Conversely, if you see a headline that says, "Big Snow Storm Coming," you are way more apt to click on that link to find out more. The TV news and newspaper have been doing this for years. The difference now, though, is instead of reporting the news once or twice per day, it is minute by minute. Each station keeps up with every change in order to be the first to report. What about the TV shows/movies we watch? All of them compete to get you to watch them, too. So, each show or movie needs to become more outrageous in order to get you to watch, right? *The Walking Dead, Game of Thrones, Grey's Anatomy*—all of them go over the top to get you to watch AND tune back in next week!

Everyone is fighting for the real estate in your head. So, they will do so with every means necessary.

Allowing negative speech, thoughts or visions into your head makes no sense. Unfortunately, in the name of being entertained, we often allow ANYTHING to come inside our brain without regard for what it could do to us. "It's just a TV show," we'll say. "It doesn't change how I think, feel or act." I disagree, and it has been proven to be true. The things that go into your brain have a massive influence on your life.

What are you listening to?

1. Books
2. Podcasts
3. Music

What are you watching?

1. TV Shows
2. NetFlix/YouTube
3. Social Media

If you put yourself in the wrong place, you are going to be at risk for receiving something negative. If you go to a fast food restaurant, you are in danger of eating crappy food. If you go to a party you shouldn't be at, you're more likely to do things you don't want to. If you watch a show or listen to music that is not congruent with the way you want to live your life, then you are likely to start thinking or acting in a different way.

Chapter 7: Focus

Be mindful of everything that is going on around you. Make sure the environment around you is rich, fulfilling and uplifting consistently. Don't put yourself into positions where you are likely to get pulled down. Choose wisely who you allow into your circle of influence.

Here are some basic thoughts:

* Be mindful of everything going on in your head.
* Hold every thought captive.
* Don't allow the negativity to grow.
* Test your thoughts against your standard of truth and see if they measure up.
* If your thoughts don't lead you to positive action, change them.
* If you think about positive things, then you will continually have positive actions.
* Do you have a standard that you test your thoughts against?

Do you have statements to which you can refer back to that will center you in times of difficulty? Former All-Star pitcher and Mental Skills Coach, Bob Tewksbury, calls these anchor statements. In his book, ***90 Percent Mental: An All-Star Player Turned Mental Skills Coach Reveals the Hidden Game of Baseball,*** Tewksbury talks about how he used anchor statements on the mound to prevent him from allowing negative thoughts to impact his performance.

Before a game, he had a specific routine of phrases he would repeat or meditate on to get his mind focused. If he allowed a home run, he had simple statements that he repeated in his head so he could get back on track as soon as possible. We need to employ these statements, too. These positive thoughts are ones you can go back to when you are having a negative thought or moment. You may not be a major league pitcher, but you certainly know that if you allow a negative thought to manifest in your mind, it can have a huge impact on your day. If you make a mistake, do you talk down to yourself? Do you call yourself stupid or think what a dummy you are? Instead, have pre-planned anchor statements that you can repeat when you need them the most. They are there when you have a bad day, make a mistake, or something outside of your control happens. If you don't find a way to pull yourself back to center and get rid of the negativity, it is going to be a long day for you and everyone around you. Learn to hold those thoughts captive, test them against the truth, and get rid of anything that is going to slow you down.

The key to getting your mind right is to consistently have positive people and positive messages going through your mind. In order to do that, you first must take an inventory of where you are and what is currently going on in your head and with your life.

Chapter 7: Focus

Recap:

Who do you allow to have a positive impact on your life?

_____

_____

_____

Are there people you need to spend less time with in order to achieve your goals?

_____

_____

Are there people your need to spend more time with in order to achieve your goals?

_____

_____

What are you listening to or watching that needs to go because it is not a good influence on you?

_____

_____

What do you need to listen to or watch more of because it is a positive influence on you?

_____

_____

Do you have positive anchor statements that you go back to in times of trouble or when negativity pops up?

_____

_____

Chapter 8

Living with Intentionality

"Live your life on purpose."
—Unknown

"BUSY" HAS BECOME A buzz word in our culture. It is the first response to every conversation. It usually goes something like this…

Me: "How are you doing?"

Almost everyone: "Busy. The kids have X going on, work is hectic, and we are just busy!"

We are always busy. Between work, the kids, marriage, friends, family, we are unable to do anything else because we are so busy. Unfortunately, we use this as a status symbol and a crutch.

Chapter 8 : Living with Intentionality

It's a status symbol to be in such "demand" that we are busy. We want to feel validated by the pace of our schedule in order to show others that we are important or to keep up with the everyone around us. It is also a crutch, because we allow our busy-ness to keep us from things that are truly important.

Busy is a disease of the mind. It clutters and prevents us from being our best and keeps us from focusing on what is truly important. One of the biggest problems often lies in that we are uncomfortable saying "No." We don't want to disappoint anyone or make it look like we don't have it all together. So, we live life at a frantic pace trying to keep up. Meanwhile, we are alienating the people we love the most and not doing our absolute best with the work we were created to do.

If you want to live with intentionality, then you need to do a couple things.

1. Start with the end in mind
2. Set your goals and systems in place
3. Live a proactive, action-oriented life
4. Do what you said you would do

Start with the End in Mind

Did you accomplish all your goals last year? The answer is probably not. We often get to specific times like the end of the year, a birthday or anniversary and think, "I expected to be a lot further along than I am at this point."

We get frustrated because we are off target. The problem is that most of us don't know what target we are aiming at. We want to get healthy, be happy, have fun, but we have no specific marker for success. Even if we have an end point in mind, we generally don't take our current situation into account before we set a goal, so we have no idea if it's truly attainable.

So, to make this year different, we are going to start with the end in mind. At the end of this year, what do you want to be true of your life? Is it a specific weight, job, location? Do you know where you want to be in three, five, ten years? Do you know what you want people to say about you when you die? (I know, it's slightly morbid to think about what people would say about you in a eulogy, but seriously, what would you want people to say?)

Whatever you want to accomplish this year, you need to start living your life according to those ideas. Really take the time to think about what is important to you and where you want to go, then you can start setting your life up accordingly. Starting with the end in mind can start to help you not only establish goals, but also to set up the systems in your life that will allow you to achieve long term success.

CHAPTER 8 : LIVING WITH INTENTIONALITY

Set Your Goals and Systems in Place

"...We can do anything, but not everything."
KEVIN PLANK, CEO, UNDER ARMOR.

I often try to be the hero. I take on too many responsibilities and try to do too much. Some of this is born out of a generous, helpful place. Most of the time it's because I want to help, be a blessing to others and relieve their burdens. But if I'm honest, sometimes it's because I want to be the hero. I want the credit, want to get a project done in a specific way and make sure everyone knows I did it. Thinking and acting this way are harmful to me and others around me, though. It too often prevents me from dedicating more time to areas of my life that are strengths and suppresses the growth of others. It also means that I might not be getting the best work done. Do you understand what I mean?

I know that I am not alone in this. Understanding our priorities and working on those specific things would benefit all of us. In order to be better spouses, parents, leaders, business owners, employees, healthier people, we should learn to say "No" more.

If we said "No," we would be more likely to excel in the areas where we were created for and not get bogged down in the junk we shouldn't be doing anyway! Saying "No" means that we have to get rid of our ego. It sounds easy, but we know it's not.

Saying "No" means you have to be fully connected with your purpose. If you are clear on your purpose and mission, you will know the actions required to make that purpose a reality. Having that clarity will provide you with direction. That means if someone asks you to do something, you will have a specific, personalized guide to help you answer. Saying "No" to a non-priority will allow you to say "Yes" to a priority.

Think about it. If being a good father or mother is a priority to you, then does your calendar reflect that? Do you carve out the time necessary to spend the quality time with them that they need in order to develop that relationship? Do you say "No" to events that will take you away from your kids? If you want to lose weight, do you have your workouts and meals planned before the week begins? Do you say "No" to late nights out in order to say "Yes" to early morning workouts? Don't be so willing to say "Yes" to someone or something that isn't a priority. Don't neglect the work you were meant to do. Say "No" more.

"That's not a priority to me at this point."

Saying "No" isn't always easy but saying something is not a priority to you at this point shows real intentionality. "I don't have time," is a statement we all use, but it's not true. We all have the same 24 hours. If you are not getting something done, then it is clearly not a priority. **What gets prioritized, gets done.** If you want to lose weight, then getting to the gym and eating better, should be a priority. That means your calendar should change and you need to automatically schedule your training and eating. Don't leave it to chance. If you know at the end of the day there is a possibility you might cancel your workouts because you get tired from work, then go first thing in the morning. This way, you no longer say, "I don't have time," you MAKE time. Prioritize the important and learn to say "No."

Live a Proactive, Action-Oriented Life

My wife is the queen of calendars and organization. Seriously, she has electronic and paper planners, highlighters and color-coordinated schedules. She has a lot of responsibility, so it is a part of her routine to make sure that she stays on track and knows exactly where we all have to be at all times. I am SO grateful for her. Me, on the other hand ... not so much. I try. Actually, it is #2 on my priority list. In order to maximize my potential and live a full life, I need to be better at understanding what my priorities are and where they go in my calendar. I know I need to put the kids' events in the calendar FIRST, so I don't end up overcommitting and missing something. I need to schedule my workouts for the week so that I don't neglect myself and stay on track with my goals. One of the ways we have started to work on that is by having a meeting every Sunday morning to set up our calendar for the week. We go through day by day so we know what events are happening that week and where our priorities are so that we can achieve our goals. This shift has dramatically helped me be proactive and has given me the freedom to do the things that are important to me, because I know when and where I need to be most of the time.

By prioritizing the important, you are making a choice to live intentionally. In order to live intentionally, you will need to organize your life in a way that allows you to live proactively. It means you prioritize your calendar by setting up your week in advance, understand your Top Three Actions for the day and know when to say "No."

Living a proactive life is simple, but not easy. Setting up regular check points with yourself and others can help you stay on track to achieve your goals. This will require you organizing your calendar. It may mean that you will have to sacrifice one thing to invest in another, but in the end, if you know what is important to you, then you will know exactly what to do. Now you just have to do it!

Do What You Said You Would Do

Each New Year, many well-intentioned people set up their New Year's Resolutions to make big changes. We build the perfect plans, set up the right diet, work to get the new job and more. Unfortunately, 80 percent or more of those resolutions are broken. Sometimes it's because we chose a plan or path that wasn't good for us, but often, we just don't do what we said we would do.

We have come to expect this. We often accept the excuses from ourselves and others, but that is not living an intentional, proactive life. Doing what you said you would do is called integrity. Your word is your bond. If you say you are going to do something, you should do it. If you are clear on your priorities, then you know when you can say "Yes." If that is the case, then you just need to show up and do what you said you would.

Chapter 8 : Living with Intentionality

Jim Rohn said, "We all must suffer from one of two pains: the pain of discipline or the pain of regret. The difference is discipline weighs ounces while regrets weigh tons." If you said you were going to get up and workout at 5 a.m., do it. The pain of waking up early is way easier than the regret of not going and trying to fit it in later. If you miss that session, it may throw off your whole day. I see this all the time with my clients. They negotiate with themselves that they will go later in the day so they can sleep in now, but ultimately, they have something else that keeps coming up and prevents them from coming in. That little negotiation—the choice to sleep or work out—often leads people to get off track. Those little decisions turn out to be big deals later. Do what you said you were going to do. The pain of discipline is way easier to take than regret.

Recap:

Are you a people pleaser?

_____

Do you often want to be the hero?

_____

What do you need to say "No" to more often?

_____

_____

Do you need to reorganize your calendar?

_____

Do you have your goals and systems set up to guide your life?

_____

Are you living proactively or reactively right now?

_____

Do you take action on the things that are important to you?

_____

Are you living with integrity?

_____

Do you do the things you said you would do?

_____

_____

_____

Chapter 9

Choose Your Attitude

*"Your attitude, not your aptitude,
will determine your altitude."*
—Zig Ziglar

EVERY TUESDAY, I TAKE the garbage out at my house. We have three growing boys, and so each week, we have a pile of garbage and recycling. It is critical that we take the garbage out each week! If we don't, we end up having a pile of bags waiting to fit into the garbage can, or we have to try to stuff it down. As I took out the garbage today, I was filled with gratitude that I could get all this junk out of my house. I was happy to get rid of the crap so that I have a chance to start over for the next week.

Each day is a new opportunity. When you wake up in the morning, you have the chance to do something that has never been done before. It all starts with your attitude, though. There is no way you are going to have a positive day with a crappy attitude. It's not possible. Every morning I begin my day by giving thanks to GOD for the new day and the opportunity ahead of me. Sometimes it is a long prayer, other times it's short. It can be done through worship music, meditation, journaling, gratitude or exercise. I believe that it is the best way to start the day.

Whether you believe in GOD or not, going through a routine in the morning to center yourself will be crucial to success. Living intentionally requires that you wake up and live purposefully, choosing how you will view the day. Will you choose to let the stress and worry of yesterday run your life? Are you prepared for what is going to come today? You cannot prepare for everything, but what you can do is get your mind focused on what is important and choose the attitude you have going into the day.

I think there are a couple of specific ways we should think when it comes to our attitude.

Be Positive

Author Ben Hardy wrote, "In 2005, the National Science Foundation published an article showing that the average person has between 12,000 and 60,000 thoughts per day. Of those, 80% are negative and 95% are exactly the same repetitive thoughts as the day before." That means that we have to be intentional with the way we think. If we aren't, we will think the same thoughts as yesterday, which are likely to be negative. Thoughts become things.

Whatever you are thinking is going to come out in your actions. Positive in means positive out. This means feeding yourself positive information consistently so you can develop your positive outlook.

Whether it's reading the Bible, meditating, listening to books or podcasts, and watching motivational material, focus on making everything you consume be positive. Zig Ziglar has a quote on motivation that I live by. He says, "People often say that motivation doesn't last. Well, neither does bathing—that's why we recommend it daily." Fill your mind with positivity. Although bad things will happen in your lives, being intentional starts with CHOOSING what goes into your brain regularly so that you can live your best life and be a beacon of hope for others. Your good attitude can influence others and have a huge impact. When storms come, you can be the pillar that they lean on because they know you are filled with good thoughts and are mentally strong. Conversely, when you need lifting up, others will remember how your positivity helped them and they will be a support for you.

Be Grateful

Gratitude is a key component to a great life. A 2009 study by the National Institute of Health showed that the hypothalamus fires up when we perform an act of kindness or when we show gratitude. This is important because the hypothalamus is responsible for appetite, sleep, metabolism, body temperature and more. Also, when we feel gratitude, we get a dopamine release in our brain. Dopamine is a neurotransmitter that is responsible for feelings of satisfaction and pleasure. It is a "reward" in our brain. Living a grateful life creates a physiological impact.

In addition, it is hard to be angry and grateful at the same time. It is hard to be jealous and compare your life to others when you live in a constant state of gratitude. Living consistently in a state of gratefulness will change your life. We live in a world where comparison rules. We are constantly told that we need the newest car, gadget or clothes. Comparison is the thief of joy. Stop living a life where you are trying to compare or keep up; rather, live life with gratitude.

If you can read this then you have something for which to be grateful. List off the things that bring you joy; the challenges you have made it through, the people that support and encourage you and the gifts you have been given. Can you walk, talk, have food to eat, a roof over your head or clothes on your back? From the big to the little, we can choose to be grateful. Choose to not live a life of comparison.

Ed Mylett has a saying he uses called Blissful Dissatisfaction. Basically, he is saying that right now, you need to live a life of joy and gratitude. Regardless of your situation, choose to be grateful, so that you can be whole as a person. We all want to achieve more, but if you don't live in gratitude right now, then when you achieve your goal, you will still be unhappy.

One truth I believe is that you are enough, where and who you are right now. You don't need anything to complete you. Period.

Hard stop. We hear this message of "get better" or "be the best version of yourself" and we start to think that we are not enough as we currently are. You can be enough and want to be better at the same time. Being confident doesn't require faking it until you make it. You are it, right now. If you are faking it, how are going to be genuine when you "make it?" Faking it also can prop you up into arrogance rather than having genuine confidence in who you are. Choose right now to be confident in your strengths, be aware of your weaknesses, and know that you were uniquely created to bring gifts to this world. Be joyful in who you are today and strive to grow into the best version of yourself!

Be Present

"Yesterday is history, tomorrow is a mystery, today is a gift, that's why it's called the present."
—Unknown

On my iPhone, I have this tab under Settings that says Screen Time. It is one of the things that I would least like for people to see. At the end of the week, I get a report that tells me how long I have been on my phone. Too often, it is ugly. Like, I could have driven from New York to D.C., or worse. When I stop to think about what that means, I get frustrated. It means I probably robbed my wife, kids, employees, friends and others of the best of my day because I wasn't intentional with my time.

We live in a distracted world. There are so many things that are competing for our time and attention. Being present takes a tremendous amount of intentionality. It also will save you a significant amount of time and energy. Gloria Mack is a professor at the University of California, Irvine, and she studies digital distraction. Her studies have shown that it takes, on average, 23 minutes and 15 seconds to return your focus to a task after a digital distraction. Seriously! The lesson to be learned? We lose too much time being distracted!

We go to Facebook, Instagram and Twitter to be entertained. That means whatever is going on in front of us is not as entertaining as what *MIGHT* be happening on the internet. When we look at our phone, TV, iPad or computer, it tells anyone around us that we are not interested in them and think there is something better going on elsewhere. That can be really discouraging and defeating, especially if you have kids.

This is why being intentional with your mind is incredibly important to ultimately becoming your best version of yourself. Abraham Maslow said, "The ability to be in the present moment is a major component of mental wellness."

If you want to live your best life, you need to work to be present more often. When we are fully engaged with what we are doing, though, we don't get distracted. Being present puts you in tune with what is going on around you and allows you to soak in the moments that will create memories. When you are present, you will be a better listener, retain more information, and you will connect more with the people who matter—the ones that are right in front of you.

Set up rules for your life such as, when you get home you will put your iPhone away until the kids go to bed or turn off the internet for periods of time. Find ways to be more present and intentional and your relationships and productivity will skyrocket!

Recap:

What do you need to STOP doing in order to be more positive?

_____

_____

Do you need to change your environment, friends, etc.?

_____

What do you need to start doing in order to increase your positive thoughts?

_____

_____

What can you listen to, watch, or do more of to be positive?

_____

_____

_____

Chapter 9 : Choose Your Attitude

What are you grateful for?

_____

_____

Do you have a journal that you write in to document your gratitude?

_____

_____

What steps do you need to take to be more present?

_____

_____

Do you have a strategy for your screen time?

_____

_____

_____

How can you reduce the amount of time you spend on your devices?

_____

_____

_____

_____

Chapter 10

Choose Your Actions

"Your direct actions, not thoughts, will define you. Direction, not intention determines your destination."
—Andy Stanley

BEING INTENTIONAL WITH YOUR attitude is the first step of the process. It is the foundation. Your actions are, ultimately, what you will be known for. Here are four things you can do to develop better action skills:

Be Disciplined

For the moment all discipline seems painful rather than pleasant, but later it yields the peaceful fruit of righteousness to those that have been trained by it. (Hebrews 12:11, NLT)

As a society, we have lost our ability to be patient. We want everything done right now. If we need an answer to a question, we

Chapter 10 : Choose Your Actions

can ask Siri or Alexa. We also have access to just about anything we want at any time—food, clothes, electronics, and everything Amazon Prime has to offer (which is *EVERYTHING!*).

Talking about discipline is about as fun as getting a root canal. We don't want to have to eat well, get up early, work out, save money or do anything that requires us to delay gratification.

But we admire people that do. Think about the athletes we idolize. We want to play basketball like LeBron, be a quarterback like Drew Brees, and hit a baseball like Bryce Harper. We want our favorite team to win championships—but that requires a lot of time and effort. It is the training in the offseason that we don't see that makes all the difference. The hours in the gym and on the court or field that makes the difference.

We certainly want our kids to be their best. We want them to work hard, get good grades, and practice hard at sports, music or theatre, but we don't demonstrate to them the actions they REALLY need. Often, we don't show them how to be disciplined.

Training to be disciplined is difficult, no doubt about it. It goes against everything that is within us. But, when you train yourself to be disciplined, your life will bear significant fruit. Delayed gratification will provide you with long term satisfaction and happiness. Choose to do the hard things now so that you can achieve the goals you have later!

Discipline begins in the mind. It takes time to think about your goals and priorities, so that you can establish patterns in your life to make them come true. Setting up a schedule requires that you reverse-engineer your life to achieve your goals. This means setting up bed time and a waking time, eating times, working times and deadlines. It will also mean putting in time to NOT work. When are you going to spend time with your spouse or significant other? Are you going to have lunch with your kids once a week, or take them to school? When will you go on vacation? This type of thinking will allow you to spend time on the important things and make sure that the work you put in matches the results you desire.

Discipline is "tough" stuff. It requires that you quit negotiating with yourself, train your brain to do what is important to you and then follow through on that. Consistently. If you establish patterns and rules for your life, you will achieve more and have the chance to maximize your potential. Choose to be disciplined.

Be Relentless

"You just can't beat the person who never gives up."
—BABE RUTH

I grew up a Chicago Bulls fan in the 1990s. IT. WAS. THE. BEST. All they did was win championships. As a fan, I had so much fun watching those games. But before the '90s, the Bulls were not a great team. I was reminded of that not long ago when I watched a video describing the failure of the Bulls and Michael Jordan against the Detroit Pistons in the late 1980s.

Chapter 10 : Choose Your Actions

The Pistons were known as the Bad Boys. They were tough and mean, physically beating on opponents during games. This was a strategy they employed against the Bulls and particularly against Michael Jordan. Coach Chuck Daly decided to not let Jordan single-handedly defeat his team, so they just bullied him. Mentally, physically, emotionally, the Pistons just wore him down. For three years the Pistons defeated the Bulls in the playoffs to knock them out, twice in the Eastern Conference Finals.

Jordan became relentless in his pursuit of beating the Pistons. He was determined to get over the hump. In the midst of getting beat, Jordan decided to change his approach. He hired a trainer named Tim Grover to help him get stronger so that he could withstand the beatings he was taking. Grover worked with Jordan not only to get physically stronger, but to get mentally and emotionally stronger. The strategy worked as Jordan and the Bulls swept the Pistons in 1991 on their way to their first championship.

Challenges are going to come your way. Tough times, difficult decisions, and challenging people will try to derail you from your dreams. This is why having a purpose is critical. Your purpose will drive you. If it is deep enough, it will allow you to be relentless in the pursuit of your dreams. Being relentless means that you don't quit in the face of adversity. When a challenge comes, you won't back down. When you make a mistake, you will correct and start moving forward again faster. If one path closes, you find another one.

We often give up too easily. Think about what being relentless means to you and how it will impact you and those around you. What behaviors are your demonstrating to your spouse, kids, family, friends and community? Are you the type of person who is resilient in the face of challenges, or do you give up at the first sign of difficulty?

Begin to develop the habit of being relentless. Don't be willing to quit or cave when things get tough. Fight for what you believe in with all you have. Be relentless in the pursuit of the things that are important to you.

Be Learning

The active pursuit of information and knowledge is the key to continuing to develop into your best version. We live in the information age. We don't lack for the ability to learn how to do anything. Seriously, if you want to learn a new subject, develop a new skill or understand a topic better, Google it. If you are interested in a topic, start to move in the direction of that subject. Really dig into it. Find books, articles, podcasts or anything that is associated with the topic and start devouring the information. Find out who the thought leaders are in that field and start to research what they are reading, writing or saying. There is so much information out there that is free or inexpensive that there really is no reason to not be able to grow every day.

Chapter 10 : Choose Your Actions

Reading

Readers are leaders. If you want to grow, you should be reading. Whether it's books, newspaper, articles, blogs, find the resources that line up with what you are trying to learn and consistently read them. Find thought leaders in a specific area and follow their blog, see who they are following and what information or ideas they are talking about. It will give you an insight into what they think is important and how it can help you continue to progress on your path to mastery.

Listening

Some people will say they don't have time to read. First of all, that is baloney. They haven't made it a priority. Another way to learn, though, is to listen. Audiobooks, podcasts, motivational speeches are all great ways to expand your horizons. As with the books, find people who are leading the charge on a particular topic and follow them and who they are listening to. Don't waste an opportunity. If you know you are going to be driving, set up your "Automobile University," as Zig Ziglar said. The car is a great time to learn, especially if you are living a life that is busy. Use those moments to learn in order to keep growing.

With technology and the accessibility of information, not growing is a choice. Continuing to learn is what it takes to grow and become the best version of yourself. It allows you to continue to fill yourself with positive thoughts and gives you the capacity to do more than you could ever do before.

Be Action Oriented

"We'll take it."

When we were opening Movement Fitness, we worked through a great deal of information and planning in a short amount of time. It took less than three months to go from beginning discussion to LLC with a full business plan. It happened fast. What was even scarier, was that we were searching for property with our business partner prior to having funding. We were negotiating with two properties. One we loved and another that would work but was not ideal. In the meantime, we were working with two banks to receive funding that would allow us to open our doors. Prior to receiving official word regarding our funding, David said we needed to take the ideal property. I was scared OUT OF MY MIND! Seriously, the what-ifs were running rampant in my mind. It was nerve-wracking, but he was right. It was time to go.

"I can't start. I'm not 100 percent ready!" Have you ever thought this to yourself or said it to someone else? We are waiting for just the right moment, enough money or for the perfect sign that we are supposed to go. We want the assurance that we are doing the right thing. The truth is, if you are waiting for perfect, you will never get anything done. Start right now. You may not be able to do everything you want today, but you can start. We often

Chapter 10 : Choose Your Actions

get paralyzed because we want to move mountains but don't know how. You were not made to move a mountain. You were made to take steps. If you continue to take steps, you will be amazed at what will happen in a relatively short period of time, IF you just keep going. Yes, there are times for contemplation, but all in all, we spend too much time thinking about what we should be doing. Just start moving. Motion creates emotion! Take action and start moving in the direction of your dreams today.

Chapter 11

Go to Bed!

"One of the great responsibilities that I have is to manage my assets wisely, so that they create value."
—ALICE WALTON

I WORKED AT MENARDS for a year during college. Menards is a Midwest hardware store, similar to Home Depot or Lowe's. It was also nicknamed "hottie heaven" because of the cute girls that worked there. It was a great experience! I loved working there for a few reasons. They paid me $2.50 more per hour on the weekend, and I got to drive a forklift! Also, it was where I met my wife!

One of my favorite tasks was cleaning up and organizing a storage area outside in the lumber yard. Our space in the lumber yard allowed us to keep our excess products stored away from our department until we needed to bring them in to restock. Because of the demands of the store, though, it made the management of

Chapter 11: Go to Bed!

this area difficult as we were constantly moving products in and out.

This was where I first learned about taking an inventory. On most Saturdays, my boss would hand me a list of things that needed to get done; what products were low on the shelves and what products needed to get moved off the shelves and into storage. This tedious task was made more fun because I drove the forklift to move and organize all of this stuff. We had a few aisles that were consistently messed up during the week trying to keep the shelves stocked, so it was my job to organize the area, and get stuff in or out depending on the season. It was a great job, but it wasn't always easy or fun.

Taking a personal inventory isn't always fun. It means that we have to dig into ourselves. We have, to take the time to evaluate where we are in order to move forward so we can become the best version of ourselves. It's not about beating yourself up or creating frustration. It's about finding out where you are today so that you can begin to make the changes that are going to help you in the long run. It's important to start RIGHT NOW by analyzing where you are so you can start to organize your life around the priorities.

The easiest way to begin evaluating yourself is taking stock of your days.

What do you do each day? Look at your habits and see if they are helpful or harmful. You can start with this list:

1. Are you happy with where you are? _____
2. Do you get 7-8 hours of sleep each night: Y   N
3. What time do you go to bed? _____
4. What time do you wake up? _____
5. How many times do you hit the snooze button? _____ (really)
6. How many hours do you spend at work? _____
7. How many hours do you spend with family? _____
8. How many meals do you eat per day? _____
9. When do you normally eat? _____
10. How many workouts per week? _____
11. How many hours do you spend on social media each day? _____ (if you don't know, look at your settings and it will tell you.)

The fastest way to change your life is to change something you do daily. Author John Maxwell said, "The secret of your success is determined by your daily agenda." Once you understand where you are, you can start setting up the systems necessary to help you become your absolute best!

Sleep

People often ask me what the best diet, supplement or weight loss strategy is and the first thing I tell them is sleep! **Start with**

Chapter 11: Go to Bed!

sleep. No matter who you are, what career you have, sleep is an integral part of living a healthy lifestyle. Yes, I understand that there are times when you will have less sleep, but those should be the exception to the rule rather than the standard. Not getting enough sleep on a regular basis is a choice. There is one exception to that and that is parents of infants.

If you are the parent of an infant, you are in a season of life where you might not be getting much sleep. I understand. Do your best. Give yourself permission to take naps when available. Go to bed earlier, if possible. At this stage life can be difficult, but it doesn't have to drive you nuts. Be grateful for what you have and do your best to get rest.

For everyone else, sleep is a **PRIORITY,** and we need to start treating it like one. We are often mindless about our sleep until we get to the point that we're desperate for it. Sleep is such an important part of being our very best. *Do not neglect this area of your life.* I understand there will be times when we will not get the perfect amount of sleep, but those should be seasons and times rather than a way of life.

Poor sleep is responsible for a significant amount of health issues including:

1. Obesity
2. Heart Disease
3. Mental Fog
4. And more

But really, it will keep your from living your best life! Your overall energy and ability to achieve your goals will be significantly decreased if you don't get enough sleep.

Evaluate how many hours of sleep you currently get. What time do you turn the phone or TV off and go to sleep? It will be an adjustment if you are used to going to bed with a TV or phone, but you need to put them down and go to sleep.

We can make a significant impact on the quality of our lives, the interactions that we have and the work that we do if we get the proper amount of sleep. Ask yourself these questions. If you get enough sleep are you:

1. A better father, mother, wife, husband, son, daughter or friend?
2. Able to do better work for your job?
3. Able to have more energy, exercise more and overall, be healthier?

I guarantee you are a better person if you get the sleep you need.

The formula for sleep is simple:

(Wake-Up Time minus 7 or 8 hours) = Bed Time!

Sleep Debt

The recommendation for sleep is 49-56 hours per week, which breaks down to 7-8 hours per night. We know that not every night is perfect, so if you are unable to get the nightly recommendation, then you can make it up later in the week. The problem comes when sleep debt is accrued, and we cannot overcome it. Chronic issues are created or exacerbated by a lack of sleep. Sleep time is similar to money. The more debt you build up, the harder it is to overcome. Stay consistent and be intentional with your sleep. Taking the time to plan out your nightly habits can make a significant difference in your life.

A great bedtime routine begins by going backwards. What time do you need to wake up in the morning? Knowing when you are going to wake up, you subtract 7 hours or more from that number and that is the time you should be going to sleep each night. It is a simple formula, but if you don't regularly monitor the time you go to bed each night, you could easily find yourself with sleep deprivation. Given the importance of sleep, set a reminder in your phone one hour before you need to go to bed so you can mentally prepare.

I think we made it clear that you need 7-8 hours of sleep each night, right? For some, not getting enough sleep is a result of a choice; for others, the struggle to get sleep is real and causes major issues. Sometimes it is necessary to get medical help for sleep, but before you go to the doctor for help, try evaluating the following.

Sleep Hygiene

One area of sleep that is often overlooked, though, is sleep hygiene. Look at the conditions in which you sleep every night and ask yourself the following questions. Is your room…

- √ Completely dark?
- √ Quiet?
- √ 60-67 Degrees?

Get Rid of the Light

One of the first tips in sleep hygiene is eliminating the light that is in your bedroom. You want to make sure that you get the room as dark as possible so you cannot be disturbed by ambient light. Get your room as dark as possible to maximize sleep. Here are a few ways you can do this.

1. Blackout Curtains
2. Sleep Mask
3. Removing Lit Objects from the Room
4. Switching Rooms

The easiest and quickest way to remove light is to buy a sleep mask. They are cheap and will make your room dark because of the covering of your eyes. They can be a game changer. For about $10-$15, you can remove the light from any room. It may take a little bit to get used to and they are not always perfect, but if you get a good one, it can have a huge impact on your sleep quality! For those of you that don't want to sleep with a mask on, the next best option are blackout curtains.

Blackout curtains are a GREAT option but can be expensive depending on the size of your room. If you are looking to upgrade, then you can use this as your sign to do so, but they are very nice and can help to make a dramatic change in the lighting of your room.

Another important room rule is to get rid of devices with a light. First off, your phone doesn't belong in the bedroom, so get it out (more on that in a minute). Find another alarm clock to wake you up. If you have an alarm clock, or any other device that has light, turn it face down if you can't move it out of the room. This will make a significant difference. I have an alarm clock on my watch that is my first alarm clock and a second digital alarm clock in my bathroom that goes off just after the first one. This makes sure I get out of bed in the morning.

Also, turn off the TV. Sleeping with the TV on is a great distractor from sleep. While the noise may "help" you get to sleep, I would bet that in a short amount of time you would be better off using a sound machine or just getting rid of sound altogether. It will prevent you from getting to that deep REM sleep you need.

Get Your Phone OUT of Your Room!

We have become connected to our phones almost 24/7. There is probably nothing that costs you more time than scrolling through your phone. We are all guilty of it at different times. If you sleep with your phone within an arm's reach of you while in bed, your quality of sleep is significantly less than it should be. Get your phone out of your room; that way, you are not tempted to get on it, or be awakened by the buzzes, dings and whistles of your phone.

Here's a great tip—put a reminder in your phone for one hour before you go to bed. When that timer goes off, that's the time you should put the phone down for good as well. If you don't, chances are, you will end up scrolling mindlessly through your Facebook, Instagram, ESPN or Pinterest apps. There is a reason why the phone is hard to put down. The blue light that is emitted is designed to draw your eye and adjust your circadian rhythm. It makes your brain think that the sun is still out and that it is okay to be awake. Even if you are looking only for a moment, it can take up to 23 minutes for your brain to adjust and for you to shut down and get back to sleep.

If you are using your phone as an alarm, then it is time to get a new alarm clock. Just because your phone CAN do everything, doesn't mean it SHOULD. Go buy an alarm clock. Put it in your bathroom or just outside your bedroom, while you put your iPhone in another room far away. If you set your alarm clock, with your alarms outside your room, it will help you get out of bed. That annoying alarm is going to keep going until you get your butt up and turn it off. Then, the second alarm is in another room, and that will go off just a couple minutes after the first. This is a great strategy to stop hitting the snooze button and get out of bed every single day.

Reduce Distracting Noise as Much as Possible

Reducing the sound in your room as much as possible is another way to improve your sleep hygiene. It allows your brain to turn off and get to the deepest levels of sleep possible and necessary. Turning off the TV, radio (or your *snoring spouse)* will be a huge benefit for you. Because these are varying levels of noise, they can impact your quality of sleep. Reducing the amount of noise in your room can make a big difference when you are sleeping. Early in the sleep cycle we especially want to remove any barrier to a deep, satisfying sleep. Ear plugs are a great way to reduce the amount of noise in the room, especially if you live in a city or somewhere with extra noise coming in. Another great option is a white noise machine, a fan or air purifier. These devices provide a consistent noise that can overcome other, more disruptive noises.

Room Temperature

According to the National Sleep Foundation, 60-67 Degrees is the ideal temperature range for going to sleep. As we go to bed, our body temperature decreases in order to initiate sleep. Making sure your room is set to this temperature will help you get into a deep sleep sooner. If you are too hot or cold, it can keep you awake longer and disrupt the early stages of sleep which make it a problem for a satisfying sleep.

Write to Sleep

Have you ever had one of those nights when you are tired and can't wait to get into bed? Imagine, you crawl into you bed ready to shut off the day, get some sleep and start over tomorrow. Ahh. Good night. You close your eyes and all of a sudden, your brain starts swirling with ideas and thoughts that you can't turn off. You think about things that happened today or something that is coming up in the future that has you stressed, worried or hopeful you don't forget. You try as hard as you can, but you can't shut off your brain.

Stress is a major issue for many when going to bed. If you had a long day or a stressful situation occur either at work or home, then it can be a problem for you to go to sleep. It is difficult to turn off your thoughts and emotions sometimes.

We can't always alleviate stress prior to going to bed. What you can do, though, is set yourself up to have the best scenario possible. If your brain is constantly churning, one suggestion is to find a way to get those things out of your head. One thing we can start doing immediately is to write ourselves to sleep. A study by Michael Scullin, published in the *Journal of Experimental Psychology*, recommends writing as a way to get to sleep faster. It helps by removing all the unfinished tasks from your brain. This practice is simple. Just take a piece of paper and start to write out all the things are inside your head. Yes, I said ALL the things that are inside of your head. If it's in your head, write it down on paper. Whether it's good, bad or otherwise, write it down. This habit will help you start to let go of your stress at bedtime, because you have addressed it, knowing you will come back to it in the morning or give it the attention it deserves later. You may also learn that it doesn't matter, and you can let it go! Consistently doing this will give you a release to go to sleep, but it will also help you to organize the next day, so that you can be prepared to hit the ground running tomorrow.

To-Do List

Once you have everything out on paper, the next step is to create a to-do list. If something is not important, then you can let it go, but if it needs action, then you can start to put that into an organized plan for tomorrow. Creating this list can help provide clarity and give specific actionable items to get done. Did you forget to do something today? Put it in your calendar for tomorrow. Do you have an event coming up and you have work to do in order to prepare? Create a list and start to map out a timeline to complete. Need to have a conversation with a friend or co-worker? Schedule time to book a lunch or coffee. Putting these thoughts into specific times and dates can not only help to prepare you for what is coming, but also can create clarity around what is important. If it is not important or not one of your priorities, then give it away or let it go. Also, creating timelines can help provide a sense of urgency and turn your list from a bunch of stuff to do into actionable items that will receive the attention they need.

Action List

Creating the to-do list is great, but if it stays just a long list of stuff to do, then it can be VERY overwhelming. Instead of leaving it that way, we are going to create an Action List.

Take your to-do list and start to pull off the priorities you need to take action on tomorrow. This will help you determine what is truly important and give you actionable items so that you start accomplishing the important things in your life! Doing this consistently will help you to get more done and will also help you to stay on track with the priorities in your life!

Setting Yourself Up for Sleep

We are going to implement a specific strategy for preparing for bedtime, so we have fewer restless nights and wake up filled with energy. We are going to implement the 8-2-1-0 plan. This is an adapted version of Craig Ballantyne's 10-3-2-1-0 Plan. It goes like this:

8-2-1-0 Plan

In order to get the best night of sleep possible, we need to set ourselves up for success. Energy is created by the body when we fuel it and recover well. So here are some simple, yet important things to help you go to sleep faster and wake up more refreshed in the morning.

Chapter 11: Go to Bed!

8 Hours Before Bed: No More Caffeine!

I love caffeine, like most of us. I have coffee in the morning and use Advocare Spark to provide me with energy. Caffeine can be a great addition to your day if you use it wisely. According to the Mayo Clinic, the maximum recommended daily amount of caffeine is 400 mg per day. One Starbucks Venti Blonde coffee has 475 mg! We often overutilize caffeine, which makes us stay up later, deprives us of our sleep, then requires us to DRINK MORE coffee the next day to make up for it. It is a VICIOUS cycle!

So here is how we are going to combat that. We are going to decrease the amount of coffee that we drink and begin to rely on sleep and nutrition to give us the energy that we need in order to BE OUR BEST! The first step—stop drinking coffee when we are close to going to bed. Eight hours before you go to bed, STOP DRINKING CAFFEINE. If you are going to bed at 10 p.m., that means 2 p.m. is your last caffeine for the day! For some of you, this won't be a problem. For others, this will be a big shift. It might take you a few days to a week to adjust, but I promise you it will work, and you will be less reliant on caffeine long term if you do this! Whatever your bedtime is, eight hours before bed, put a reminder in your phone—no more caffeine.

2 Hours Before Bed: No Food

The goal here is to create the MOST optimal way for you to sleep! Heavy digestion can prevent you from getting that DEEP sleep that you desire. Plus, eating too close to bedtime can provide

ADDITIONAL calories that will keep you from your weight loss goals. For most of us, eating within two hours of bedtime is not positive, so let's stop it.

EXCEPTIONS: If you have a job that keeps you from eating until late, you CAN eat, as long as the calories you are consuming are within your daily calorie intake. This is not permission to overeat, but it is making sure that if you have an atypical schedule, you are getting the nutrition you need.

1 Hour Before Bed: No More Screens

Do you know that your iPhone or Android device is MEANT to draw your eyes? People work to figure out how they can get you to look at a video, an article, post and then get you to look at the next one, and the next one …

The blue light emitted from the screen is designed to draw your eyes in by mimicking the sun's rays. Put the phone down, and read a book, talk to your spouse, partner or kids. Find a way to begin a new process of winding down.

Maybe for you, the phone isn't a problem. Maybe it is the TV! No screens means no TV, too! If you are falling asleep with the screen on, you are NOT getting the best sleep possible. It's okay to watch a show, but if you are binge-watching Netflix, then you are likely to do a couple things:

1. Overeat

Chapter 11: Go to Bed!

    a. You're just sitting there, bored, watching TV, so grabbing a snack is easy. A little one won't hurt, right? Wrong; those late-night calories are sneaky and will add up on you REALLY quickly!

2. Stay up later than you want

    a. Have you ever thought, "I'm going to get up early and work out, or go to work early?" You have great intentions, but most of the time you don't get up. You are relying on WILLPOWER, and when you don't get up, you think you are weak or "I'm just not a morning person." The truth is that you are not aligning your actions with your priorities. What gets prioritized gets DONE. Getting to sleep will start your day strong and help you MAXIMIZE your productivity. It will also make you ready to go to bed the next day!

3. Create movement issues

    a. If you are sitting on your couch, La-Z-Boy or chair, you are, for sure, not in the best physical position. Most likely you are slouched over or lying in a less than optimal position. You are better off going to bed, reading for a bit and then falling asleep.

4. Not thinking

    a. Really, watching TV is mindless. Think for yourself and grow your knowledge with something that is stimulating your brain. When was the last time you read a book? Really? If you want to get better and reach your full potential, then you need to think for yourself and challenge yourself with new concepts.

5. Overwork

   a. We work too much. Seriously. I understand there are seasons of life where we are busy, but those should be SEASONS, not lifestyles. We often end up in emergencies because we don't take the time to plan and schedule our workout OR we give our bosses and co-workers the ability to access us at any time. If you put down the email at 7 or 8 p.m., you won't miss out on communication. Try it. If it is an emergency, it won't (or shouldn't) be sent through an email. If an email is sent to you late at night, let it go. If you respond at 10 p.m. or 7 a.m., it won't make a difference for that person, but it will make a difference to you. Shutting down the email/work, will give you the peace of mind to turn off your job for a bit and train people you work with to realize your job is NOT your life. It is a part of it, but not the whole part. This will be difficult at first, but it will be freeing in the long run.

One hour before you go to bed, put a reminder in your phone to turn OFF the screens!

Chapter 11: Go to Bed!

0: The amount of times you are allowed to hit the snooze.

You know hitting the snooze button is not good for you. You THINK it feels good in the morning to hit the snooze, but really, you know it's not. It causes lethargy. You keep putting off getting out of bed for some reason.

If you have GOALS to achieve, then hitting the snooze button is DEADLY. You are telling your dreams they can wait, because you want five more minutes of sub-par sleep.

If you really want five more minutes of sleep, go to bed five minutes earlier at night and then you can truly get a RESTFUL five extra minutes.

An easy way to avoid this is to stop using your smartphone as an alarm. Put it in another room and use an actual old-fashioned alarm clock. This will force you to get out of bed to turn it off and it is harder to get back into bed once you are up! Do whatever you need to, but in the morning, don't hit the Snooze!

If you don't know when you are going to wake up, then hitting the snooze button isn't a big deal. But really, if you are hitting the snooze button, you are telling yourself that ten minutes of poor sleep is more important than getting up and spending time on something that is worthwhile.

NO MORE!

Ten minutes doesn't seem like a long time, but added up, it can make a huge difference. Over the course of a year, it adds 48 hours. You can do some significant work with that amount of time over a year. Waking up at a consistent time can set you on a path to becoming a master of something of personal interest.

You will first have to create this discipline, but once it becomes a habit, it will be easy, because your purpose will get you out of bed.

Get your butt out of bed the FIRST TIME the alarm goes off!

Another way to help you get out of bed is no more scrolling! One of the biggest time-wasters now is social media scrolling. One of the worst times for this is during the morning when we wake up or before we go to bed. We use our phone as our alarm clock, because we want to make sure that we are never too far from the phone. We keep it on our night stand, and as soon as the alarm goes off, if we don't hit snooze the first time, we grab the phone and start scrolling through our social media. Facebook, Instagram, Snapchat or LinkedIn—it doesn't really matter, we just want to scroll. It's a way to "wake up" now. We know that everyone puts their best foot forward on social media, so when you see the perfect life others are leading, it can make you feel like you are "less than." The more you put the phone down, the more you will realize you don't need it. This is another reason to get your phone out of your bedroom. It is totally weird at first, but you will get used to it. Find a place in your house to put your phone when you are home. This is a great way to reduce your phone usage when you are home, anyway, so you can engage more with your family or those that are over. Setting up a docking station in a room of your house that is not a central room will prevent random scrolling and will help you to get out of bed

Get an alarm clock that you put somewhere that forces you to get out of bed. Put it in your bathroom or across the room—just put it somewhere that will make it difficult to get back into bed. This is one of those things that seems silly, but if you do it, it can help you begin your day with purpose.

Get Dressed

Since you are already up, get dressed. This is another layer to your morning routine that will make it difficult to get back into bed.

It will also help you to prevent rushing around later in the morning. We want to set up our mornings to help us to prevent haste and frustration. If you are up, dressed and ready to go, it will significantly reduce the risk of having to rush.

Engage Your Brain

The next step to a great morning is to engage your brain in a proactive way. Rather than using the news or social media as your engagement to start the day, we need to find a more productive way to get us thinking and moving. Here are some great ways to begin to get your mind focused on the important.

1. Prayer
2. Devotional
3. Meditation
4. Journaling/Writing

Regardless of your beliefs, all of the above work to cultivate an attitude of gratitude. These can help you to stop focusing on all that is wrong or stressful and remind you to start with being grateful for all that you have.

One of my favorite pieces of scripture that is paramount to my faith and setting up my day is Romans 12:2, "Do not conform to the pattern of this world, but be transformed by the renewing of your mind."

As a follower of Jesus, renewing my mind every day is a major part of living an authentic and genuine life. If you get stuck in your negative thoughts, you need to find a way to get rid of that. I use scripture and motivational messages to help me set up my day well, and also help me to get out of what Zig Ziglar calls "Stinkin' Thinkin'!"

If you want to transform your life, you must first start by transforming your thoughts!

Eat Well

There are a number of studies that look at when you should eat. You can cut the data in a number of ways, but let me ask you, when you eat a good breakfast, do you feel better? Are you satisfied throughout the beginning part of your day? Do you make it to lunch with less temptation to eat junk food or extra unnecessary snacks?

I would bet the answer is yes. You *can* choose to not eat breakfast, but is that the best choice? So often we don't eat a good breakfast because we are late and running frantically trying to get somewhere on time. This leaves us feeling grumpy and likely to eat more than we should and make poor food choices.

Breakfast is essential for productivity throughout the course the day. If you eat breakfast, you will have a significantly higher chance of being satisfied, and you're going to be able to make it through the first part of your day without that mental fog of hunger.

So, find what works for you and do it. If your mornings are busy, grab a shake that is quick, easy and has the nutrition you need. If that doesn't work, then make a quick breakfast or eat something you prepared the night before. Planning is important and will set you up for success.

Chapter 12

Nutrition

"Let food be thy medicine and medicine be thy food."
—Hippocrates

IMAGINE YOUR BEST FRIEND comes to you and asks you for advice. They want to lose weight and they need help. What would you tell them? Even if you don't have a degree in nutrition, your advice would probably start with eating veggies and fruit, eat protein and cut out the fatty and sugary foods. Right? That seems simple. Too simple. But it is a solid starting point.

Food and nutrition are some of the MOST debated and talked about topics in our country today. Nutrition is confusing, and I get so many questions about it.

What diet should I be on?

Should I do Keto?

CHAPTER 12: NUTRITION

I've heard counting macros is good, should I do that?

Is intermittent fasting the best?

Even though every one of those questions is well-intentioned, it is the wrong place to start. These questions invoke the desire to change a strategy, not a lifestyle. The real question isn't what diet works best, but rather what works best for **YOU**! Every diet has been proven to work in some way. Intermittent fasting, paleo, low-carb, Dukan, vegan, and more are all diets that have been shown to help people lose weight. And here is the truth—they all work. The bottom line is they all cause a calorie restriction in some way. The techniques might be different, but all of them restrict you in some way.

All the information that is available makes nutrition extremely complicated, but it doesn't have to be that way.

If you want to:

Lose weight: Burn more calories than you consume

Maintain weight: Burn the same calories that you consume

Gain Weight: Consume more calories than you burn

That's it. It's simple, but not easy.

We want nutrition to be complicated, because if it is complicated, then it's not our fault. If it is complicated, we don't have to take action, because we're confused. Complicated gives us the permission to stay stuck. You don't need more information, what you need is action. *Doing* is the key to success. Start with what you know and do that. When you know better, do better. Here is the hard part—being *consistent* with it. I would love to tell you that your journey will be a linear line and there won't be any bumps in the road, but that's just not true. Difficulties will come at you, and they will mostly be self-inflicted. If you want to change your relationship with food, it starts with your mind. You have to get motivated and stay motivated to make a change, and then be committed to consistent action.

Preparation

Preparation is the key to almost anything in life. When we look at our favorite sports teams or musicians, the difference between good and great is in the preparation. For some, planning provides the shackles that constrain their freedom. For others, it motivates them into inaction. The point of preparation is knowing where you are going to go and planning in advance what it will take to get there. For example, if you prepare your food in advance for the week, it should prevent you from going off your plan while saving you time, money, and energy. If you want to lose weight, or achieve a certain goal, then this is the best way to achieve it. Don't switch it. If you need help, tell someone that you know will hold you accountable to it. You took the effort to make this meal, eat it. If it's not good, eat it anyway, then figure out how to make it better next time.

Chapter 12: Nutrition

We get frustrated with preparation because it isn't glamorous and takes time. Setting your intentions or menu is a key part of success. If you don't know what you are going to eat, you are setting yourself up for failure. If you get hungry and don't know what you are going to eat, then you are headed for disaster. Being unsure of your goals and what you what to achieve will leave you on a never-ending journey. Make sure that you set up check points along the way so that you know where you are going and to make sure you are on the right track. Take the extra time to write, think and plan so that you can achieve your goals.

With that being said, here is some specific advice that will help you start to take steps to get better today:

Eat Breakfast

Breakfast is often overlooked because we hit the snooze button. It leaves us grabbing something as you walk out the door or hitting the drive-thru for a coffee and a bagel. You know this isn't a great start to the day, but because there wasn't a plan, this is what you're left with. The fact that the day started poorly means eventually, you are going to run out of energy and be hungry. That is a bad combination. It leaves you looking for food in a hungry state, knowing that you need to get something in your body soon. Bad choices arise. You snack too much on cheap foods, or eat a massive meal filled with things you don't need.

Start planning your breakfast the night before. I believe breakfast is the most important meal of the day for one reason.

If you start off your day wrong, the likelihood that you are going to go off the rails is significantly higher. You're either likely to be hungry sooner or if you are asked to lunch, there is a tendency to say, "I already had a donut for breakfast, might as well have (fill in fast food place) for lunch and start over new tomorrow." Get rid of that mentality.

I think breakfast is the most important meal of the day. It sets the intention for how you are going to spend your day. If you begin eating a bagel, you are more likely to cut another corner the rest of the day. Be intentional with your breakfast. This is the tone-setter of the day. This is a chance to declare your intentions and start in the right direction. If you don't start well, you are more likely to have some junk snacks in the mid-morning and/or have a huge lunch that you eat on the run and has little nutritional value to us. Choose to start your day well. If you eat a good breakfast, it is significantly harder to make the choice to eat fast food for lunch.

Every morning, I have my Advocare Muscle Gain Shake, with peanut butter, banana, milk and chia seeds. I put some ice in, blend it up and it tastes better than any milkshake—really. I partner that with my Advocare Reds, and my vitamins. It takes about ten minutes to complete the whole process. My wife does an Advocare Meal Replacement Shake each morning, because with three boys, she doesn't have time to have a sit-down breakfast. Regardless, we set up our bodies for success by starting off with the right nutrition.

CHAPTER 12: NUTRITION

Preparing and eating a meal in the morning can be difficult, that is why I choose a shake. If you would rather eat whole food, that is great, just don't eat the typical American breakfast. Our breakfasts are usually filled with SUGAR! Get rid of the orange juice, bagels, donuts, cereal and anything else that is loaded with sugar. If you eat that, it is a sure way to start crashing at work or school during the mid-morning. The best breakfast includes protein, fat and some carbs.

You can find recipes at www.begreattodaybook.com. There are also tons of great recipes out there. Find a couple you like, keep it simple and use those in the morning. Don't make it complicated, pick something and start your day off right!

Lunch

One of the single biggest ways to save time, calories and money is to pack your lunch. Lunch can be a costly time. If you choose to go out to eat, you are automatically at risk for consuming more calories. Even if you pick the "healthy" choices at restaurants, you are still likely to overeat. The calories of the meals are always higher than what we think and sometimes we have no clue what the calories are, and that is a bad sign. This leads to overeating. The problem with eating too much at lunch is that it leads us to being full longer, which often prevents us from eating dinner until later in the evening, or even not at all. This cycle of not eating breakfast (or not a good one), eating a poor lunch, not eating dinner until late, or eating no dinner and just excessive snacking at night leads us down the path of continual weight gain. This combination will make you gain weight, leave you crabby with no energy and affect your sleep. It is a vicious cycle that repeats itself over and over, until we wake up one day looking in the mirror thinking, "How did I get here?"

These poor patterns can be avoided with just a little extra work. On Saturday or Sunday, find time to make five meals that will last you for lunches throughout the week. Meal prep doesn't have to be a three-hour marathon. It can be as simple as cooking some protein, dividing it into containers, chopping up vegetables and fruit and pairing those with some fat. For example, cook up chicken or turkey, and split it into 4-6 oz. containers. Then, cut up some broccoli, and fruit of your choice, add a serving of almonds, and that's it. If that doesn't interest you, make a turkey wrap with cheese, rather than a sandwich (less carbs than bread) and pair that with carrots and strawberries. Maybe make a great salad that doesn't have a ton of dressing on it. There are so many lunch combos that don't have to be boring. Find something that works for you and make them for the week, so you are prepared! Choose to take the extra time on the weekend to set yourself up for success. This small step will help save your waistline and your overall health.

Dinner

"What's for dinner?" is one of the most dangerous questions! Think about it. Usually it results in a Ping Pong match of, "I don't

CHAPTER 12: NUTRITION

know. What do you want?" between two people. This often leads to "Forget it. Let's go out to eat." And that leads to overeating and overspending!

Dinner can be tough. You have a busy day at work, come home, work on homework, take the kids to practice and get everything ready for tomorrow. It can be stressful. It won't be easy to eat at home with good food that helps you move closer to your goals, but it will be worth it. Preparation is the key to getting and staying ahead.

A few years ago, as the pace of our lives picked up with kids, activities, and owning a business, my wife started planning out our dinners for the following week. She gets the recipes, puts the ingredients on the shopping list, and then will organize them in the refrigerator accordingly. This strategy takes some planning on the front end, but it saves us so much when it comes to making dinner that day. It prevents the risk of making something our family won't eat, and it reduces the risk that we will guess what we are having for dinner and make a poor choice in the moment because we are hungry.

Planning out in advance what you are going to eat for the week can make a huge difference in staying on your track with your food goals. Before you go to the grocery store, choose seven recipes that you enjoy and put those ingredients on your shopping list. Along with the meals you are going to prep for lunch and breakfast, it may take a few more minutes to prepare your shopping list, but it will save you time, money and calories throughout the course of the week. Having your shopping list done in advance will help you to buy exactly what is needed and reduce the risk of over-buying and having too much food in your fridge, or under-buying and having to go back to the store later in the week.

Be intentional with your time so that you can avoid getting frustrated and off track.

Be Prepared

For all your meals, start by setting yourself up well. Tomorrow morning, are you going to make a healthy shake for breakfast or have eggs and oatmeal? Either one is a great option, but make sure you get up in time to make the meal and make sure you have all the ingredients. There is little that is more disappointing than planning and then realizing that you don't have what you need to follow through on it.

Each night, you can also set up your lunch by packing one for the next day. If you are unsure what to pack, here is how you can set yourself up well:

* Take a wrap instead of a sandwich
* Pack vegetables and fruit
* Bring the leftovers from your dinner last night
* Also, you could meal prep food on Sunday

Any of these options will set you up for success.

Chapter 12: Nutrition

James Clear, author of the book, ***Atomic Habits***, writes, "You do not rise to the level of your goals. You fall to the level of your systems." When taking an inventory, evaluate where your systems are and how they can improve to help you achieve your goals. Be disciplined with your time and effort, and you will find that it will create MORE freedom and time!

Chapter 13

Get Moving

*"The mind, body and spirit are all closely connected.
Be careful as they will all catch the disease of the other."*
-Dr. David Jeremiah

I HAVE A SKETCHY memory of my youth. I really don't remember a lot, but the things I do remember are etched into my brain. When I was 12 years old, I watched Conan the Barbarian at my Uncle Mike's house. I'm not sure why or how I watched the movie, but after watching it I became a fan of Arnold Schwarzenegger. Building and developing muscles become a primary life goal for me. I was fortunate that around that time, our junior high basketball coach and PE teacher started teaching weightlifting at school. I LOVED IT! I put together a bench set out of milk crates in my parents' garage and used my dad's Ted Williams plates. These things were plastic filled with concrete.

Chapter 13: Get Moving

There was nothing sexy about them, but I used them anyway. I was an athlete, and I was determined to make it to the major leagues. I thought this would be a way to help me to do that. Plus, I wanted to look good for the girls. I found that if you put in the effort, you could get stronger. I didn't have a philosophy of training then, but I did have a desire to be better than everyone else on any athletic field I played on.

Exercising has helped me in every single area of my life. The principles of exercise, particularly strength training, for me, have been critical in my personal development. They have helped me learn the value of Consistency, Commitment, and Overcoming Challenges. These things are a central theme for progressive exercise and for our life.

Here is what I want you to know: Many of you reading this might not love exercise. You might hate the idea of doing something physical, especially on a daily or regular basis. You may not understand my desire, or why building muscle and working out is so important to me, but I want to tell you a couple things.

1. Nobody LOVES to work out everyday
2. Exercise shouldn't be a punishment
3. It isn't easy, but it is so worth it
4. It's more than vanity

Nobody loves to work out everyday

I work out early on most mornings. Four days a week, I am on the elliptical at 4 a.m., and one day I am in the gym early for strength training. When I was bodybuilding and had a different schedule, I was in the gym five-six days per week at 5 a.m. There is one reason I started going to the gym that early in the morning—rarely is anything else competing for my time.

If you get up and get moving, you are setting an intention for the day that you have prioritized your health first, in order to be the best version of yourself. You don't have to work out that early. You just need to find something that works for you.

That being said, I don't love to get up and workout every morning—especially getting on that elliptical! UGH! Seriously, it is not the first thing that I want to do. But, because I have mapped out my purpose and mission, being healthy is a priority in my life. I choose to work out because I know what it is like to be overweight and unhappy with who you are physically. I know first-hand that the pain of discipline is much easier to take than the pain of regret.

The biggest reason is I don't want to live my life with regret. It is probably the thing that I am most afraid of. So, while I don't always love to work out, I do love what it does for me. It is a switch for my mental state. It gets me moving and thinking and that creates a change of mindset. It puts me in a better place. I can get bogged down in work, writing, leading, trying to grow a business, have a family, etc. But, EVERY TIME I train, I FEEL better. I get my brain unjammed and the blood flow makes me see more clearly and pushes me to start moving. We spend so much time inside our heads that we get stressed, worried, fearful, and then stuck.

"The real reason we feel so good when we get our blood pumping is that it makes the brain function at its best," says Dr. John Ratey, Associate Clinical Professor at Harvard Medical School. "The point of exercise is to build and condition the brain." He also says that, "Inactivity is killing our brains."

So instead of thinking about "not loving" each individual workout, think, instead, of what the process of exercise can do for you over time. Think about how it will make you a better person and help those around you. Know that your ability to move is a gift that needs to be celebrated and taken advantage of. It's simple, but not easy!

Exercise isn't a punishment.

Using exercise as punishment is dangerous. This type of mindset not only potentially damages your body, but really is a symptom of a negative mindset. You need to get rid of these stinking thoughts. Don't punish yourself for what you ate last night or what you have been eating. If you ate poorly, the first step is to stop eating that way, and then yes, you should go work out, but not because you need to undo what you did last night. Go exercise because you can. Do your best with what you have, where you are, right now.

Celebrate that your body can move and be grateful for that. My goal would be to have you fall in love with the process of working out and getting better every single day! Exercise is not just good for the body, but it is good for your mind, too.

Executives from major companies like Richard Branson, Virgin; Tim Cook, Apple; Mark Cuban, Dallas Mavericks, and more all have a training routine. Tim Cook wakes up at 3:45 a.m. to head into the gym. Richard Branson gets up at 5 a.m. to play tennis, or even kitesurf, and Mark Cuban plays basketball and does Latin dance classes, all while being able to bench 300 pounds.

These people use exercise as a method to maximize their physical bodies and to help their mental skills. They don't punish themselves. They find ways to use their bodies in activities that often are fun and allow them to be their best. It keeps them physically capable of doing their job, but also allows them to be at the top of their game mentally.

In his book, ***Spark: The Revolutionary New Science of Exercise and the Brain,*** Dr. Ratey says that exercise makes you more alert, creative, motivated, and perceptive. "It's helping you learn better, remember more, and combat stress. It's boosting your mood while helping you overcome anxiety and depression."

Not only is working out good for your body, it fights heart disease, obesity, and more. It also creates new brain patterns and helps to develop better mental health in the long run. This clarity can help you when you are feeling stuck, frustrated or defeated.

Chapter 13: Get Moving

It will change your mindset and give you an opportunity to reset. I don't know of anything else that will change your mental state faster than working out.

So, allow exercise to help you maximize your life, not be a punishment. It will be far more likely that you will sustain a good exercise routine if you stop thinking negatively about it.

It isn't easy, but it is so worth it.

There are a lot of ways to exercise. The key is to find something that works for you. It needs to fit your body, schedule, and meet you where you are. It might not be the same always, but don't get bogged down in that. Get into a community of people that will support and love you for who you are, right now, and that will help you get to where you want to go. If you are a self-starter and can find a plan that suits you to work out at a big facility, great, start doing that. If you have no idea where to start and the idea of working out in front of people is horrifying, then find a small studio that will provide coaching for you. If you already have a membership, start using it again, today.

Make it a priority in your life. Schedule it at the start of the week and stick to what you said you were going to do. It can be hard to get your workouts/training sessions in if you don't schedule it. Remember, prioritize what's important. I understand it can be hard to get up early, stop in the middle day, or go to the gym after work. But here's what I know—your life will be better if you do it.

Moving in some way every single day is going to be important. Not every day has to be a killer workout, in fact it would be detrimental. What you do need is to build consistent patterns.

First, before you begin any exercise routine, consult your physician. Get a physical and your lab work done. Self-awareness is the first step to growth.

Next, you need to begin on a plan that will help you to build the habits and patterns that you can sustain over the long term. Don't start with the most difficult things possible, or even return to the last type of exercise you were doing. Start taking small steps that will allow you to build consistency, rather than extremely hard workouts that leave you too sore to go back the rest of the week.

For more on workouts, visit www.begreattodaybook.com.

It's more than vanity.

I believe you were given the body you have for a reason. I don't know what that reason is, but I know there is one. Rick Warren, Pastor of Saddleback Church and author of ***The Purpose Driven Life*** has a quote that I love concerning our bodies, "God created it, Jesus died for it, the spirit lives in it, I'd better take care of it."

We often dismiss the connection between our mind, body, and spirit. If we are unhealthy in one area of our lives, it is HIGHLY likely that it will impact every other area of our life. Not always, but most often. Think about it; if you are not feeling good about

Chapter 13: Get Moving

yourself physically, are you likely to be willing to take a risk, go confidently to a job interview or even get off your couch some nights? You know this is true. If you are not physically where you want to be, it will negatively impact EVERY area of your life.

On the other hand, if you are feeling good about yourself, making progress and happy with how you look, you are likely to go try and conquer the world. Your mindset matters, but so does your body. They work together. Make sure you are moving and keeping yourself as healthy as possible. It is not about being "Johnny or Suzy six-pack." You don't have to have the perfect physique to be healthy, but you do need to be active. Do not let this area of your life go by the wayside. If you do, it will impact everything!

Here is another reason I believe that taking care of our body matters.

I believe you matter to GOD. He loves you so much that he sent his only son to die for you. I know he wants the best for you, even if you don't know or love him right now. I think he has a purpose for your life and wants you to be physically able to fulfill your mission. Faith and health are closely connected. Your health and body matter to GOD.

Regardless of your faith, if you want to be a person who is making a maximum impact, you need to be healthy. Do your best to take care of your one and only body.

For more on being healthy and workout plans, visit www.begreattodaybook.com.

Chapter 14

Take Action: Now

"Inaction breeds doubt and fear. Action breeds confidence and courage. If you want to conquer fear, do not sit home and think about it. Go out and get busy."
—Dale Carnegie

TWICE A YEAR, I meet with an incredible group of fitness professionals to discuss business, training and personal development. As I was preparing to go on one of our retreats, a friend of mine sent me a message. He is a successful entrepreneur, and he gave me the best advice. He said, "Don't just take notes, put stuff into your calendar for one week, two weeks, a month, a quarter that are realistic goals for those deadlines."

His quick text was a huge lesson for me. It is the key to making an actual change in our lives. It's reading a book, listening to a podcast, going to a retreat and then DOING something with

Chapter 14: Take Action: Now

the information we receive. We are so consumed with gaining information that we seldom DO anything with it. If you want to accomplish a goal, then you need to take action. Set goals with deadlines that are appropriate so that you can grow.

The first part of this book was designed to give you the motivation and inspiration to change your state of mind, so that you can start implementing a strategy that will work for you. We need to start moving! It won't be perfect, but that is not the goal. The goal is progress. Start right now, with who you are, where you are, with what you have now. Then, when you know better, do better. That's it. Don't be afraid to make mistakes, because that is where you learn. The one thing that I have found is that the more I try, the better I get. Those that are super successful have attained their success because they have dared to try new things, get outside their comfort zone, and work to be their best, even when they don't want to.

This won't be easy, but it will be so worth it. Your life will change, but isn't that why you bought this book? Over time, your purpose will adjust and adapt. Good. That means you are growing. Develop the rhythms and patterns in your life that will allow you to learn new information, DAILY and then take action on it so that you can get better and grow.

Be intentional with your attitude and your actions so that you truly can start to live your best life, one that is filled with passion, making an impact, and purpose, to transform your life and the lives of those around you.

Be Great Today 28-Day Guide

In order to make a change in your life, you have to change two things:

1. Your State of Mind
2. Your Strategy

The first part of this book is designed to help you change your state of mind. This is the most important first step of true change. If you aren't in the right state of mind, it doesn't matter how good of a strategy you put into place; it won't take effect because you are not ready to really implement the changes. Living a proactive, strategic life will require effort, planning and organization, but it will also lead you to achieve more than you ever thought possible! First, make up your mind that you want to change, then set up ways to help you KEEP that motivation over time.

Next, this 28-day plan is designed specifically to give you the strategy to create true life transformation that will last! We don't want to just achieve one goal, we want to transform your life, so you continue to live a life of intentionality and purpose over the long term, not just a quick fix. This plan is meant to help you make changes that will impact you now, and also build the schedule and priorities that will create lasting change. It will allow you to build the SYSTEMS in your life that will track progress, monitor your success and course-correct when you get

Chapter 14: Take Action: Now

off track. If you want more information or resources, you can go to www.begreattodaybook.com.

So, before you begin, I want to tell you something—if you take this seriously, it WILL change your life. YOU CAN DO THIS. YOU WILL HAVE SUCCESS. Also, you will 'fall off" at some point; that's okay. The goal is progress, not perfection. We only fail when we give up. So, when you fall off, get back up AS SOON AS POSSIBLE! Don't wallow in a "failure." Get back on track at the next available opportunity. You have 86,400 seconds in a day and each one of them is a chance to get it right!

Over the next 28 days, we are going to build a progressive plan that will ultimately allow you to build the patterns and habits in your life to achieve success. We are going to help you create success quickly, while also working to educate and motivate you to be your best over the long term. Each day, we are going to provide lessons or activities that will help to create clarity in your life, direct you to your purpose and give you the tools to begin living your best life.

Digging deep into who you are will take time and effort. It will require you to think and write—yes, you will need to write down your goals! My mentor, Todd Durkin, says that, "Writing creates clarity, and clarity precedes genius." If you want to be your best, you will need to regularly put pen to paper.

We also want to start moving TODAY! Digging into your purpose takes time, but we are also going to get into the habit of being an action-taker, so we will have specific things you can do each day to move you into the right state of mind or give you the tools to achieve your goals. So, let's get started!

FIRST, SAY TO YOURSELF WHAT YOU WOULD BE; AND THEN DO WHAT YOU HAVE TO DO.
-Epictetus

Step 1: Start with Why

What is your Reason for doing this? Really?

If you don't know what your purpose is, then finding your purpose just became your #1 priority. **We are going to work to identify what your reason for being and living is; write it down and keep it in front of you to remind you of why you are doing this.**

Unfortunately, most of us don't take the time to dig into finding out what the things are that drive us. We go through life without knowing what makes us tick. If you want to maximize your life, experience new things and leave a legacy, then knowing your purpose is essential.

Make sure that we are focusing on a PURPOSE, not a goal, task or event. We want to think bigger. Your "why" shouldn't be to lose weight or get a promotion. Your why should be deeper. Why do you want to lose weight or get a promotion? Why do you continue to do the things that you do? Losing weight by itself is a good goal, but what happens when you hit it? Do you keep going? Do you fall back into old habits? Getting a promotion is great, but are you ready for the additional responsibility that comes with

Chapter 14: Take Action: Now

getting that new job? Will it take away from time with your family and friends that will cause a tension in your life?

Over time, your goals will change. You will become interested in new things, change hobbies, or move to new places that create different opportunities. You may get married, have kids, or start a new business that changes the dynamics of your life considerably.

All of that should be driven by your WHY, your purpose. It will become a filter to everything that you want to accomplish. Do I take this job or move to this place? Does it match your WHY? Should I eat this cookie? Does it help you achieve your purpose? Ask questions like:

1. *What makes your soul sing?*
2. *What makes you smile? (people, places, hobbies, projects)*
3. *What are you doing when you feel most alive?*
4. *What activities are you doing when you lose track of time?*
5. *What are you willing to fight for?*
6. *To whom do you want to be a hero?*
7. *Who inspires you?*
8. *Who do you want to be?*
9. *What is your dream?*
10. *When was the last time you took action towards your dream?*
11. *What could you do right now to start moving towards your goals?*

12. *How could this year be different from last year?*
13. *If you were living your best life, what would it look like?*
    a. *in one week*
    b. *in one month*
    c. *in one year*
    d. *in one decade*

Part 2:

1. *What season of life are you in?*
   a. *Do you have young kids?*
   b. *Are you an empty-nester?*
   c. *Are you single?*
   d. *Are you looking for personal development?*
   e. *Are you needing to make money?*
2. *Is your job to be a provider for your family?*
   a. *Financially*
   b. *Emotionally*
   c. *Spiritually*
3. *What are the things you must do right now?*
4. *Despite all the things you must do, what can you start doing right now to move towards your goals?*
5. *Imagine you're 90 years old, reflecting back on your life. Of all the things you have done, what are you most proud of?*

Chapter 14: Take Action: Now

"Structure equals freedom."
—Craig Ballantyne

2. Schedule It

Structure will provide you with freedom. Yes, you may need to read that again. Structure will provide freedom! It takes discipline, but it will allow you to live a fulfilled life and maximizes your potential. If you take the time to dig into what your true purpose is, then you need to organize your calendar in a way that will allow you express your life through those priorities. This will give you the ability to stop saying "I don't have time," and begin MAKING time for the things that matter most to you. This will be the biggest factor in deciding if you succeed or not. You NEED to schedule it. Build your schedule intentionally with things like:

1. What time will you get up?
2. How long will you work on your Top Action?
3. When will you go to bed?
4. When will you work out/train?
5. When will you meal prep?
6. When will you leave for work/school?
7. When will you eat?
8. How many activities per week will you go to for your kids?
9. How often will you go on a date night with your spouse or partner?

Too often, we take most of these things for granted. They all kind of just happen to us. Instead, we want to make things happen for us. We want to be intentional. Do you know that Apple CEO Tim Cook has a calendar that is scheduled down to the 15-minute mark? Seriously! Now, some of you think that is crazy, but he is so intentional with his time (and he has people to help him, so understand that, too) that he knows where he is going to be, when he is going to eat, work out, go to sleep, down to the 15-minute mark. I'm not suggesting you start there. But it would provide you with a tremendous amount of freedom later on to know where you are and what you are going to be doing throughout the course of the day. Not to mention you would get more done, feel more satisfied, and continually stoke the motivational fire that will help you get up and do it all over again tomorrow!

> *"If you do not change direction,*
> *you may end up where you are heading."*
> -Lao Tzu

Step 3: No More

It is time to put a stake in the ground and declare war on the things that are keeping you down. It is time to say NO MORE to those things in your life, things like:

No More Junk Food (Starting Now! Don't wait for tomorrow.)

No More late-night TV or iPhone surfing

Chapter 14: Take Action: Now

No More Snooze Button hitting

No More Stinkin' Thinkin'

No More Living a Rudderless Life

No More Putting your dreams on HOLD!

Right Now, I want you to start training your brain to BELIEVE that you can ACHIEVE! You are going to start by being INTENTIONAL with:

1. Your Time
2. Your Priorities.
3. Your Thoughts

Here's what YOU are going to do. With whatever is left of today, you are going to prep yourself to get good rest and DOMINATE tomorrow! In order to start getting the most out of every day, we are going to start TAKING ACTION TODAY! You are ready to start making changes. You are going to set up your calendar to begin living intentionally and you are going to purchase a few things to help you get started.

Wake-Up Time for Tomorrow: _____ (1 hour before you leave the house or 1.5 hours if you have kids)

Bedtime Tonight: _____. (You need 7-8 hours of sleep, work backwards from rise time)

What are you going to eat for breakfast? _____

Option 1 [Shake Recipe]

Option 2 [Breakfast Recipe]

> *"Complexity is the enemy of execution."*
> —TONY ROBBINS

K.I.S.S. Strategy for Breakfast

Most of the time with nutrition, we OVERCOMPLICATE IT! Instead, we are going to simplify your choices. You have two options for breakfast. You are going to either do a shake or have a meal that is prepared the night before. This will prevent you from having the excuse that cooking takes time and the "I don't have time" baloney. You have time. It's just not a priority. Now, some of you are going to say, "I NEED MORE OPTIONS." Actually, you don't, especially in the beginning. You need to make decisions and stick to them. You get bored with food because being healthy is not a priority. If something is important to you, then you will do whatever you need to get it done. As you grow, you can find recipes, but for now keep it simple with breakfast.

1. A Shake
    a. My favorite shake recipe
        - Advocare Muscle Gain (2 Scoops male/1 Scoop female)
        - 1 medium banana
        - 4 oz. milk /2 oz. water

- Peanut butter (2 tbsp. male/1 tbsp. female)
- 1 tbsp. chia seeds
- Ice
- Blend

2. Egg White Avocado Toast
   - 2 egg whites, scrambled
   - 1-2 slices of multi-grain or whole grain bread (toasted)
   - 1 small avocado
   - 1 teaspoon lime juice
   - sea salt + black pepper (to taste)
   - parsley (optional for topping)

Pack Your Lunch

This is a huge opportunity for success! Lunchtime is so often filled with crappy fast food and last-minute decisions we later regret. If you pack your lunch, you will save time, money and a whole lot of calories. Don't fall into the trap of thinking you can go out to eat and do it healthy. It is almost impossible, even for the most disciplined. You wouldn't recommend an alcoholic walk into a bar, so why would you put yourself in a position to make a poor choice?

Here is what I recommend for lunch.

Grilled Chicken Salad Recipe

- Mixed greens/romaine Lettuce
- Grilled chicken breast (4-8 oz. grilled chicken breast)
- Tomatoes
- Broccoli
- Carrots
- Onion
- Cheese
- Oil and vinegar for dressing (or lemon juice)

The more colorful, the better. Add more veggies. Stay light on the dressing.

Turkey Wrap

1. Low-carb tortilla
2. 5 oz. of baby spinach
3. 1-2 servings of low sodium turkey
4. 1 slice pepper jack cheese
5. Mustard
6. Salt and pepper

You can substitute just about any protein and cheese. I would pair this with as many veggies and some fruit, plus 8-12 oz. of water or tea.

For more recipes go to www.begreattodaybook.com.

Recommended Purchases

Here are a few tools that can help you.

1. Measured water bottle
2. Sleep mask
3. Alarm clock

These three things will set you up for success going forward. Here's why:

Water Bottle:

Water is ESSENTIAL to making any kind of physical change. Begin by having a bottle that will help you keep track of your water intake. Water will be the thing you consume the MOST throughout this process. It will help you to have energy, improve brain function and increase overall performance. You are going to start by drinking at least ½ your bodyweight in ounces. (BW÷2 = Ounces of water goal per day). Yes, you will have to pee more, but considering your body is significantly impacted by water, we want to make sure we are constantly replenishing the stores.

Sleep Mask:

Sleep is the single biggest adjustment most of us need to make in our routine. We don't get enough rest, and it will catch up to us eventually. Most of the time, what we are doing at night that prevents us from sleeping is meaningless; watching TV, scrolling the internet, or eating. All of these things have a negative effect on our ability to achieve our goals. If you are having issues with weight, mental clarity or acute disease, then you are probably not getting enough sleep. Each week, if you are getting enough sleep, you will spend between 49–56 hours in bed. If you are missing out on this vital aspect of life, then you are not maximizing your productivity. Basically everything. Think you are the "SPECIAL ONE" that can get by with little sleep consistently? Think again! We are going to make sleep a PRIORITY! (2017 Meta-analysis European Journal of Clinical Nutrition)

You should make sure that you remove as many distractions as possible. Light is one of the biggest enemies of good, restful sleep. Your bedroom is probably not dark enough, unless you have blackout curtains, no phones or alarm clocks. You could buy new blackout curtains, but that would be a bigger purchase (if you need to JUSTIFY the purchase to someone, then you can use this as your excuse!). A sleep mask will get almost all of the light out of your eyes and help you get to sleep faster and stay asleep longer! It's a cheap and easy solution to help you maximize sleep.

Alarm Clock:

You need an actual alarm clock. Here's why: your phone is going BYE-BYE! No more phone by the bed. We are moving the phone to the bathroom, another room, anywhere but the bedroom. The smartphone has become one of the single largest distractions

Chapter 14: Take Action: Now

today. It keeps us from being more productive and prevents us from getting GREAT sleep. So, by getting an alarm clock, you will limit the risk of staying up to late surfing Facebook or Instagram or Netflix and will keep your from scrolling in bed after you wake up.

> *"Accountability is the glue that ties commitment to the result."*
> **—Bob Proctor**

Being a coach, I am a huge advocate for hiring someone for support and guidance. I think it is the best way to help provide a plan and accountability. When you pay someone, you have more on the line and more skin in the game. You are less likely to waste their time or your own when you make a financial investment.

We need to get someone that can give us a pat on the back or a kick in the pants—preferably someone who knows the difference between the two and when to give them. Whether you hire a professional or get a friend to help you, having accountability can be one of the biggest steps you can take in order to achieve significant and sustained success. If you hire a professional, they should be able to walk you through your calendar, help you plan out the important people and things in your life and prioritize accordingly.

If you choose to find an accountability partner, that's great, too. It probably should NOT be your best friend, though. Your friend is probably more sympathetic to your case than you need from an accountability partner. They love you, so they might struggle to keep you on track. They often don't want to call you out because it would be difficult on the relationship. Ideally it should be someone you don't want to disappoint!

Sometimes, we feel uneasy with an accountability partner, or they don't know what to ask to keep you on track. So, when you have the perfect someone, you are going to do two things:

3. Pick two check-in days per week

   a) Side note: choosing two days is ideal because it keeps you accountable on BOTH sides of the weekend. For example, Monday or Tuesday and Friday check-ins require that you don't go off the rails over the weekend.

4. Have them ask you the following questions:

   a) Are you on track with your goal?

      i. Be as specific as possible. If weight loss, use a number or pant size.

   b) Did you take the specific action you said you were going to? (Be specific)

   c) What do you need to change or continue to do to stay on track?

Chapter 14: Take Action: Now

Tracking Progress: More than the scale

Proven 5-Step Self-Accountability System

We have established an accountability partner to help us make sure we stay on track with our goals, but beyond that, how do we measure success on a consistent basis? What is the best way to know if you are physically going in the direction you want? We have a 5-step self-accountability system that will help you see progress in multiple ways to make sure you stay on the right track!

Scale: Remember, the scale is a TOOL. It can only give you a numerical representation of your relationship with gravity. Use it as such. It will tell you where you are, which can be a good thing, but it will not consider where you are going. Make sure that you use it accordingly. Most people make the mistake of not understanding how to use the scale. Here's the deal. If the scale drives you crazy or leads you to make poor short-term decisions (i.e. undereating during the day to try and hit a specific number the next day), then get on it less. Trying to hit a specific number daily is a short-term change mindset. We are not looking for that! We want to make a lifestyle change that will create habits we can keep FOREVER! Don't think small, think big. What is the long term? The scale provides us with data, we use it to inform us, then we move on. If you are not where you want to be, then make the necessary change to get there. Also know that two days of good eating won't cause massive weight loss! It is a great start, but we need to be consistent. Focus on doing the right things and the results will come!

Clothes: When we look at progress, one way to gauge our progress is simply this—look at the clothes you are wearing. Take notice of how they are fitting. Do they fit better this week than last? Are they looser or are they tighter? We often don't take a moment to think about how something is fitting as a way of checking our body composition. You can absolutely do body composition measurements, but for most people, using your clothes will give you enough information to know if you are getting better or not. This is a GREAT tool to combine with the scale to make sure we are going in the right direction. Your clothes will fit differently before the scale actually moves. Make sure you use BOTH to help you make decisions about the success of your program in the short term!

Mirror: The mirror is another way to gauge your success. Looking at the mirror can help you to again see progress before you may see it on the scale. Take a look at yourself at least once a week to see what progress you are making. In order to prevent potentially getting frustrated, think about how you feel you look this week versus last week. That will tune your eye to notice progress and changes, rather than just thinking about how you look overall, which has the potential to frustrate most of us from time to time.

Energy: This is important. Our energy informs us of how well we are doing with the things that we are putting into our mouth and the exercise we are putting out. If you are eating well, getting all or most of the nutrients that you need, sleeping well, moving in some way every day, then your energy should be able to support your workload throughout the day and leave you prepared to go to bed at night appropriately. Be careful of using too much caffeine or sleep aids to alter your energy. You should be able to naturally create the majority of energy that you need.

Check to see how your energy is throughout the course of the day and week. Do you drag at certain times of the day? Maybe you need to add a snack or another meal to help increase your energy levels. Are you filled with energy Monday–Wednesday, but then begin to wane as the weekend gets closer? Are you sleeping enough on the weekends, but then losing sleep throughout the course of the week? We all have rough days, but most of the time, if we get our food and sleep right, exercise multiple times per week, then we will have great energy!

Sleep: 7-8 Hours per day (49-56 Hours per week). If you are not sleeping well, start from the beginning. Double-check all steps to create great sleep hygiene. Most of the time, we can see positive changes from our adjustments. If you do that you should see improvement in your sleep patterns. If not, then you can go consult your physician for a sleep study to see if there are further problems that need to be addressed.

Be Great Today

The 28-Day Plan

Setup: Where are you?

_____

Weekly Prep:

_____

Big 5 Actions for the Week:

What are the MOST important things you need to get done this week?

1. _____
2. _____
3. _____
4. _____
5. _____

Big Calendar Events:

_____

_____

Are your meals ready? [Y] [N]

When will you work out this week? (*The more specific the better*)

   M T W Th F Sa Su

CHAPTER 14: THE 28-DAY PLAN

Day 1: Monday Motivation

You are making a HUGE change! Congratulations on taking action! Today, we are going to take five minutes in the morning to set up the day.

Self-Accountability Check-In:

Scale: What is your current weight? (Make sure that you weigh yourself in the morning, after you go to the bathroom, but before you eat or drink anything for consistency.)

Clothes: How are you clothes currently fitting?

Mirror: How do you feel when you look in the mirror?

Energy: How is your energy overall?

Sleep: How are your sleep patterns currently?

Start with Why: My purpose is: _____
_____

(If you don't know it yet, that's okay, but finding it is now your priority!)

What are your TOP 3 Actions of the Day that must be done, and when will you do them?

1. _____
2. _____
3. _____

How many ounces of water are you going to drink today?

_____

Pack Water Bottle: [Y] [N]

_____

Breakfast: Option 1 [Shake] 2[Meal]

_____

Lunch Packed [Y] [N]

Bedtime for tonight: _____

Prayer/Devotional/Meditation: (5-10 min.) _____

Nightly Recap:

Did you achieve your TOP 3 Actions?

_____

_____

What are the three things you are most grateful for? What was good about today?

_____

_____

_____

🚰 Did you drink your water?

_____

Are you prepared for tomorrow?

_____

Breakfast Prepared [Y] [N]

Lunch Packed [Y] [N]

> *"If you always do what you've always done, you always get what you've always gotten."*
> -JESSIE POTTER

Day 2: Transformation Tuesday

Your "Why": _____

Accountability Check-in: _____

Prayer/Devotional/Meditation _____

Bedtime for tonight: _____

What are your TOP 3 Actions of the Day and when will you do them?

1. _____
2. _____

3. _____

How many ounces of water are you going to drink today?

_____

Breakfast: 1[Shake] 2[Meal]

Lunch Packed: [Y] [N]

Pack Water Bottle: [Y] [N]

Write Three Affirmation Statements:

_____

_____

_____

This is often uncomfortable for most people because we are not used to talking to ourselves in a productive way. We are VERY capable of talking poorly to ourselves; instead, we are now going to speak positive truth into our own life. We are also going to write these statements as if they have already happened. This is a way we are working to create confidence in our subconscious. Here are some examples.

I am healthy.

I am a great father/mother/wife/husband.

I am making a SIGNIFICANT CHANGE in my life.

Chapter 14: The 28-Day Plan

I am a treasured child of GOD

I am great at what I do for a living.

I am proud of myself!

1. _____
2. _____
3. _____

Nightly Recap:

Did you achieve your TOP 3 Actions?

_____

_____

_____

What was good about today?

_____

_____

_____

How did you get better?

_____

_____

Did you drink your water?

_____

Are you prepared for tomorrow?

_____

Breakfast Prepared [Y] [N]

Lunch Packed [Y] [N]

Wake-Up Time: _____

Day 3: Wednesday Work

Your "Why": _____

_____

Accountability Check-in: _____

_____

Prayer/Devotional/Meditation: (5-10 min.) _____

Bedtime for tonight: _____

_____

What are your TOP 3 Actions of the Day and when will you do them?

1. _____

2. _____

3. _____

How many ounces of water are you going to drink today?

_____

Breakfast: 1[Shake] 2[Meal]

Lunch Packed: [Y] [N]

Pack Water Bottle: [Y] [N]

Plan Your Work, Work Your Plan. Setting up your whole day for success.

_____

_____

_____

_____

_____

As we have been learning, great mornings start with great preparation in the evening. Starting with the nighttime routine can have a HUGE impact on our days by getting the clutter out of our heads, writing out the list of things that need to get done, and prioritizing the most important thing you need to do tomorrow.

Unfortunately, most of us WANT to get up in the morning, but we don't sync our actions with desires. We rely on WILLPOWER to get us up, to the gym and to eat healthy. Willpower is great, but what works even better than willpower alone is to match your calendar and actions with your stated goals. If we want to lose weight, be more productive, run faster, then we want to make sure that we are getting the MOST out of our sleep.

So here is how we are going to do that. We are going to implement the **8/2/1/0 Plan.**

In order to get the best night sleep possible, we need to set ourselves up for success. Energy is created by the body when we fuel it and recover well. So here are some simple, yet important things to help you go to sleep faster and wake up more refreshed in the morning.

8 Hours Before Bed: No More Caffeine

I love caffeine like most of us. I have coffee in the morning and use Advocare Spark to provide me with energy. Caffeine can be a great addition to your day if you use it wisely. According to the Mayo Clinic, the maximum recommended daily amount of caffeine is 400 mg per day. One Starbucks Venti Blonde coffee has 475 mg! We often overutilize caffeine, which makes us stay up later, deprives us of our sleep, then requires us to DRINK MORE coffee the next day to make up for it. It is a VICIOUS cycle!

CHAPTER 14: THE 28-DAY PLAN

So here is how we are going to combat that. We are going to decrease the amount of coffee that we drink and begin to rely on sleep and nutrition to give us the energy that we need in order to BE OUR BEST! The first step—stop drinking coffee when we are close to going to bed. Eight hours before you go to bed, STOP DRINKING CAFFEINE. So, if you are going to bed at 10 p.m., that means 2 p.m. is your last caffeine for the day! For some of you, this won't be a problem. For others, this will be a big shift. It might take you a few days to a week to adjust, but I promise you it will work, and you will be less reliant on caffeine long term if you do this! Whatever your bedtime is, eight hours before bed, put a reminder in your phone—no more caffeine.

2 Hours Before Bed: No Food

The goal here is to create the MOST optimal way for you to sleep! Heavy digestion can prevent you from getting that DEEP sleep that you desire. Plus, eating too close to bedtime can provide ADDITIONAL calories that will keep you from your weight loss goals. For most of us, eating within two hours of bedtime is not positive, so let's stop it.

EXCEPTIONS: If you have a job that keeps you from eating until late, you CAN eat as long as the calories you are consuming are within you daily calorie intake. This is not permission to overeat, but it is making sure that if you have an atypical schedule, you are getting the nutrition you need.

1 Hour Before Bed: No More Screens

Do you know that your iPhone or Android device is MEANT to draw your eyes? People work to figure out how they can get you to look at a video, an article, post and then get you to look at the next one, and the next one …

The blue light emitted from the screen is designed to draw your eyes in by mimicking the sun's rays. Put the phone down, and read a book, talk to your spouse, partner or kids. Find a way to begin a new process of winding down.

Maybe for you, the phone isn't a problem. Maybe it is the TV! No screens means no TV, too! If you are falling asleep with the screen on, you are NOT getting the best sleep possible. It's okay to watch a show, but if you are binge-watching Netflix, then you are likely to do a couple things:

1. Overeat

   You're just sitting there, bored watching TV, so grabbing a snack is easy. A little one won't hurt, right? Wrong; those late-night calories are sneaky and will add up on you REALLY quick!

2. Stay up later than you want.

   Have you ever thought, "I'm going to get up early and workout, or go to work early?" You have great intentions, but most of the time you don't get up. You are relying on WILLPOWER, and when you don't get up, you think you are weak or "I'm

CHAPTER 14: THE 28-DAY PLAN

just not a morning person." Truth is, you are not aligning your actions with your priorities. What gets prioritized gets DONE. Getting to sleep will start your day strong and help you MAXIMIZE your productivity. It will also make you ready to go to bed the next day!

3. Create Movement Issues

   If you are sitting on you couch, La-Z-Boy or chair, you are, for sure, not in the best of positions physically. Most likely you are slouched over or lying in a less than optimal position. You are better off going to bed, reading for a bit and then falling asleep.

5. Not Thinking

   Really, watching TV is mindless. Think for yourself and grow your knowledge with something that is stimulating your brain. When was the last time you read a book? Really? If you want to get better and reach your full potential, then you need to think for yourself and challenge yourself with new concepts.

6. Overwork

   We work too much. Seriously. I understand there are seasons of life where we have busy seasons, but those should be SEASONS, not lifestyles. We often end up in emergencies because we don't take the time to plan and schedule our workout OR we give our bosses and co-workers the ability to access us at any time. If you put down the email at 7 or 8 p.m., you won't miss out on communication. Try it. If it is an emergency, it won't (or shouldn't) be sent through an email. If an email is sent to you late at night, let it go. If you respond at 10 p.m. or 7 a.m. won't make a difference for that person, but it will make a difference to you. Shutting down the email/work, will give you the peace of mind to turn off your job for a bit and train people you work with to realize your job is NOT your life. It is a part of it, but not the whole part. This will be difficult at first, but it will be freeing in the long run.

One hour before you go to bed, put a reminder in your phone to turn OFF the screens!

0: The amount of times you are allowed to hit the snooze.

You know hitting the snooze button is not good for you. You THINK it feels good in the morning to hit the snooze, but really, you know it's not helpful. It causes lethargy. You keep putting off getting out of bed for some reason.

If you have GOALS to achieve, then hitting the snooze button is DEADLY. You are telling your dreams they can wait, because you want five more minutes of sub-par sleep. If you really want five more minutes of sleep, go to bed five minutes earlier at night and then you can actually get a RESTFUL five extra minutes.

An easy way to avoid this is to stop using your smartphone as an alarm. Put it in another room and use an actual old-fashioned alarm clock. This will force you to get out of bed to turn it off and it is harder for you to get back into bed once you have gotten up!

Do whatever you need to do, but in the morning, don't hit the Snooze!

Nightly Recap:

Did you achieve your TOP 3 Actions?

_____

_____

_____

What was good about today?

_____

_____

How did you get better?

Did you drink your water?

_____

Are you prepared for tomorrow?

_____

Breakfast Prepared [Y] [N]

Lunch Packed [Y] N]

Tomorrow Morning Wake-Up Time: _____

Day 4: Thankful Thursday

Your "Why": _____

Accountability Check-in: _____

Prayer/Devotional/Meditation: (5-10 min.) _____

Bedtime for tonight: _____

What are your TOP 3 Actions of the Day and when will you do them?

1. _____
2. _____
3. _____

How many ounces of water are you going to drink today?

_____

Breakfast: Option 1[Shake] 2[Meal]

Lunch Packed: [Y] [N]

Pack Water Bottle: [Y] [N]

Write five things you are grateful for:

No matter what your scenario or circumstance, there is always something for which to be grateful. Seriously. Whether you are in a great place right now or struggling, using gratitude is the easiest way to change your state of mind. It is hard to be mad and grateful at the same time. If you want to make a change, start with being grateful. Whether you just got a promotion or just got laid off, if you have lungs that work, legs that move, a mouth that can eat, you have something for which to be grateful. If you have a home to live in, cars to transport you and friends and family to support you, we can give thanks.

Make sure to include:

The people in your life that are making a difference or have made a difference.

The body that you have and how it works.

The career or job that you have/school that you go to.

If you don't have a job, be grateful for the opportunity to go GET ONE. An attitude of gratitude will CHANGE your perspective and make your life more productive and filled with good things. Don't get stuck in thinking about what you *DON'T* have, focus on what you *DO* have!

Nightly Recap:

Did you achieve your TOP 3 Actions?

_____

_____

_____

What was good about today?

_____

_____

How did you get better?

_____

_____

Did you drink your water?

_____

Are you prepared for tomorrow?

_____

Breakfast Prepared [Y] [N]

Lunch Packed [Y] [N]

Tomorrow Morning Wake-Up Time _____

Day 5: Friday Focus

Your "Why": _____

Accountability Check-in: _____

Prayer/Devotional/Meditation: (5-10 min.) _____

Bedtime for tonight: _____

Chapter 14: The 28-Day Plan

What are your TOP 3 Actions of the Day and when will you do them?

1. _____

2. _____

3. _____

How many ounces of water are you going to drink today?

_____

Breakfast: Option 1[Shake] 2[Meal]

Lunch Packed: [Y] [N]

Pack Water Bottle: [Y] [N]

Friday is a difficult day when it comes to change. So, we are going to FOCUS on a very clear message. What is the BIGGEST thing you need to DO in order to set yourself up for success today and going into the weekend? Think through the following:

Are you traveling? _____

What will it take to travel well? Food/Snacks/Water

_____

How can you stay on track with your workouts/training? Hotel/ Running/Friends …

_____

Are you going to be home?

Do you have tasks/chores to do to set you up for the week ahead?

Are you behind on the work you need to do at home?

What are you going to do to prevent overeating or eating out?

Did you talk to your buddy about this weekend?

Nightly Recap:

Did you achieve your TOP 3 Actions?

1. _____
2. _____
3. _____

What was good about today?

_____

_____

How did you get better?

_____

_____

Did you drink your water?

_____

Chapter 14: The 28-Day Plan

Are you prepared for tomorrow?

_____

Breakfast Prepared [Y] [N]

Lunch Packed [Y] [ ]

Tomorrow Morning Wake-Up Time _____

Weekend Priorities:

The weekend is NOT the time to "TAKE OFF" from your plan. Unfortunately, too many of us think we do our "Main Job" throughout the course of the week. and then the weekend is a time to (fill in the blank, veg on the couch, recover from drinking, overeat …).

Here's the deal: Saturday and Sunday make up almost 30 percent of your week. DO NOT lose your progress during these two days. This is where most people struggle. You will constantly be trying to catch up all week if you don't take care of today!

So, plan your day. Whether you are traveling for a kids' event or tournament, working around the house, or hanging out with your family and friends, be intentional about what you are doing. It may be a good day to have one meal or snack that you indulge in, but don't go overboard.

Clean out Your Cupboards

Time to get rid of the junk. So, here is the deal. Go looking for the food that does not help you get to your goals. It's time to do something with it. If you can donate it to a food pantry, do that. If not, throw it away. Seriously, get rid of it. If you have junk food in the house, YOU WILL EAT IT! Why test your willpower? Remove all temptation and be done with it.

Create Your Shopping List

Here is where the victory happens.

Meal Prep is WAY more than just cooking a bunch of meals on Sunday night. It takes planning and preparation to make sure that what you are cooking is going to set you up for the week. So, here is how the best meal prep works.

My wife has the best plan that I know of to make sure that we are planned out and eating healthy throughout the course of the week.

1. Know what your breakfast is.
    a. We have been giving you only a few options for your breakfast intentionally. Most of the time, we have too many options, and then we don't make a choice and either eat something that is less than optimal, or we don't eat at all, which sets you up for DISASTER later on in the day.

    b. PICK OUT YOUR BREAKFAST IN THE A.M. AND HAVE IT LAID OUT ON THE COUNTER (UNLESS IT NEEDS TO BE REFRIGERATED).

    c. Don't change your breakfast on the fly. Have the supplies you need the night before and stick to the plan.

2. Cook two meals to prep for the week

    a. For Lunch/Snacks

    b. Cooking two different recipes that make up between six-eight total meals so that you are prepared for the week can set you up for great success this week. If you have two, you are less likely to get bored with what you are eating. You will have lunch ready to go. Know in advance if you will be able to have a microwave, or if you need a refrigerator. Think ahead to what you are going to be doing on that specific day.

3. Know what your dinner will be.

    a. Plan out your dinners for the week. Theresa goes through our calendar and looks at ball games, school events, and meetings, and plans out what we will eat for dinner each day. She often will buy the food and then separate it into specific meal stacks in the refrigerator in order to make sure all of the ingredients are ready, and then she can just grab them and start cooking. This is meal prep at its best. Plan. Prepare. Prosper!

Grocery Shopping

I get it, you're busy. We all are. So, grocery shopping is a place that a SIGNIFICANT amount of time can be made up. If you go to the store and know where everything is, don't over-purchase on a whim, and can do it in less than an hour with coupons that save you money, GREAT! If it is part of your routine that gets you out of the house and away from everyone for a period of time, great! If not, consider what will be the best use of your time. There are multiple options to help you be the most efficient.

Instacart is a GREAT option to help you shop from the comfort of your home, reduce over-purchasing on the fly and can save you time and money, all for less than $100 per year. We use it almost weekly and it is a HUGE help!

WalMart Pickup—more stores are going to the pickup style. You can order your groceries and then go pick them up without having to walk into the store at all! This is a great option as well.

Chapter 14: The 28-Day Plan

Day 6: Strong Saturday

Your "Why": _____

Accountability Check-in: _____

Prayer/Devotional/Meditation: (5-10 min.) _____

Bedtime for tonight: _____

What are your TOP 3 Actions of the Day and when will you do them?

1. _____

2. _____

3. _____

How many ounces of water are you going to drink today?

_____

Breakfast: Option 1[Shake] 2[Meal]

Lunch Packed: [Y] [N]

Pack Water Bottle: [Y] [N]

Nightly Recap:

Did you achieve your TOP 3 Actions?

1. _____

2. _____

3. _____

What was good about today?

_____

_____

How did you get better?

_____

_____

Did you drink your water?

_____

Are you prepared for tomorrow?

_____

Breakfast Prepared [Y] [N]

Lunch Packed [Y] [N]

Tomorrow Morning Wake-Up Time _____

Chapter 14: The 28-Day Plan

Day 7: Sunday Setup

Your "Why": _____

Accountability Check-in: _____

Prayer/Devotional/Meditation: (5-10 min.) _____

Bedtime for tonight: _____

What are your TOP 3 Actions of the Day and when will you do them?

1. _____

2. _____

3. _____

How many ounces of water are you going to drink today?

_____

Breakfast: Option 1[Shake] 2[Meal]

Lunch Packed: [Y] [N]

Pack Water Bottle: [Y] [N]

Nightly Recap:

Did you achieve your TOP 3 Actions?

1. _____

2. _____

3. _____

What was good about today?

_____

_____

How did you get better?

_____

Did you drink your water?

_____

Are you prepared for tomorrow?

_____

Breakfast Prepared [Y] [N]

Lunch Packed [Y] [N]

Tomorrow Morning Wake-Up Time _____

Sunday Priorities

Sundays, for most of us, should be a day of rest. For many this is a great time to recharge by getting a little extra sleep, going to church, spending time with family and friends and preparing for

Chapter 14: The 28-Day Plan

the week ahead. It is also a traditionally the most utilized time to meal prep. While you are preparing your meals for the week ahead (if you haven't done so on Saturday), set up your calendar for the week to match your meals.

1. When will you work out? M T W Th F Sa Su (Write times below)
2. What are the potential roadblocks that can take you off track?
    a. Kids' Events
    b. Work Meetings
    c. Other Appointments
    d. Social Gatherings
3. Date Nights
4. What time will you wake up each morning _____
5. What time will you go to bed _____
6. What are the 5 ACTION things you need to get done this week?
7. Accountability
    a. Partner Check-ins: _____
    b. 5-Step Self-Check: _____

If your calendar is set up, you will be in a GREAT position for the week. If you then send this to your accountability partner and/or spouse, you will also communicate it to others, who can then help you achieve your tasks and hold you accountable to what you said you were going to do!

Nightly Recap:

Did you achieve your TOP 3 Actions?

1. _____

2. _____

3. _____

What was good about today?

_____

_____

How did you get better?

_____

_____

Did you drink your water?

_____

Are you prepared for tomorrow?

_____

Breakfast Prepared [Y] [N]

Chapter 14: The 28-Day Plan

Lunch Packed [Y] [N]

Tomorrow Morning Wake-Up Time _____

Weekly Prep:

Big 5 Actions for the Week:

What are the MOST important things you need to get done this week?

1. _____
2. _____
3. _____
4. _____
5. _____

Big Calendar Events:

_____

_____

Are your Meals Ready? [Y] [N]

When will you work out this week? (*The more specific the better*)

   M T W Th F Sa Su

Day 8: Monday Motivation

Self-Accountability Check-In:

Scale: + or - previous week

Clothes: Fitting Better, Worse or Same as previous week

Mirror: Better, Worse or Same as previous week

Energy: Better, Worse or Same as previous week

Sleep: Better, Worse or Same as previous week

Don't overthink it, don't sleep on it, don't change it. You planned for this day! Go out and execute on the things you prepared.

1. Eat the meals you made
2. Train when you said you would
3. Get up when you said you would
4. Go to bed when you said you would

This is the first step. Just follow the plan. Revisit your why. You are set up for success, now go and execute it!

> *"There is no deficit in human resources;*
> *the deficit is in human will."*
> **-Martin Luther King, Jr.**

Your "Why": _____

Accountability Check-in: _____

CHAPTER 14: THE 28-DAY PLAN

Prayer/Devotional/Meditation: (5-10 min.) _____

Bedtime for tonight: _____

What are your TOP 3 Actions of the Day and when will you do them?

1. _____

2. _____

3. _____

How many ounces of water are you going to drink today?

_____

Breakfast: Option 1[Shake] 2[Meal]

Lunch Packed: [Y] [N]

Pack Water Bottle: [Y] [N]

Nightly Recap:

Did you achieve your TOP 3 Actions?

1. _____

2. _____

3. _____

BE GREAT TODAY

What was good about today?

_____

_____

How did you get better?

_____

_____

Did you drink your water?

_____

Are you prepared for tomorrow?

_____

Breakfast Prepared [Y] [N]

Lunch Packed [Y] [N]

Tomorrow Morning Wake-Up Time _____

Chapter 14: The 28-Day Plan

Day 9: Transformation Tuesday

Your "Why": _____

Accountability Check-in: _____

Prayer/Devotional/Meditation: (5-10 min.) _____

Bedtime for tonight: _____

What are your TOP 3 Actions of the Day and when will you do them?

1. _____
2. _____
3. _____

How many ounces of water are you going to drink today?

_____

Breakfast: Option 1[Shake] 2[Meal]

Lunch Packed: [Y] [N]

Pack Water Bottle: [Y] [N]

Write three Affirmation Statements:

1. _____
2. _____
3. _____

Transformation begins in the mind. Make sure today that you keep your goals and priorities in front of you! We are going to write affirmation statements specifically about your body and how you are working to be your best!

Examples:

My body is healthy and full of energy.

I take care of my body through exercise and making good food choices.

I am grateful for how efficiently and effectively my body works

Nightly Recap:

Did you achieve your TOP 3 Actions?

1. _____
2. _____
3. _____

What was good about today?

_____

_____

Chapter 14: The 28-Day Plan

How did you get better?

_____

_____

🥤 Did you drink your water?

_____

Are you prepared for tomorrow?

_____

Breakfast Prepared [Y] [N]

Lunch Packed [Y] [N]

Tomorrow Morning Wake-Up Time _____

Day 10: Wednesday Work

Your "Why": _____

Accountability Check-in: _____

Prayer/Devotional/Meditation: (5-10 min.) _____

Bedtime for tonight: _____

What are your TOP 3 Actions of the Day and when will you do them?

1. _____

2. _____

3. _____

How many ounces of water are you going to drink today?

_____

Breakfast: Option 1[Shake] 2[Meal]

Lunch Packed: [Y] [N]

Pack Water Bottle: [Y] [N]

Last week, we talked about the importance of what NOT to do at night in order to get to bed. Today, we are going to begin the WORK to make sure that we are MAXIMIZING our mornings!

We started by recommending that you get up 1–1.5 hours before you leave the house. Now, we want you to make sure that you are making the most of the morning time. Getting up early isn't easy, but when it is planned often yields the MOST productive time of work. For the most part, no one else is around, kids/spouse are asleep, there are no coworkers are around and you can be VERY productive! THIS IS A LEARNED SKILL. You don't have to get up at 4 a.m. to maximize productivity, but what you do need is to make sure that you are leaving yourself enough time to get your mind right so that you are PROACTIVE with your day rather than REACTIVE!

Chapter 14: The 28-Day Plan

What you do in the morning is about being SPECIFIC. So, we are going to make sure that we are focused and start by REMOVING things that are unproductive.

NO matter what time you wake up, here are a couple things you need to GIVE UP!

1. Snooze Button/Phone by Your Bed
2. Social Media Scrolling
   a. Facebook
   b. Instagram
3. Email
4. News

Getting rid of these things are important to help you live proactively and intentionally rather than reactively and without purpose.

Imagine this: the alarm on your phone goes off, and you pick it up off the nightstand. There are one of two ways this is going to go.

1. You hit snooze, roll over and wait for the next time it will go off.
2. You will scroll through social media and get lost in fantasy land for a while.

Either way, you are going to waste 20-45 minutes. Then you will rush out of bed, get dressed, yelling and hurrying the kids, all while being frustrated because you got up late! (Not that I have ever done that!)

This scenario sets EVERYONE up to fail! You make everyone upset, you eat poorly, show up to work late (or barely on time) and you are already living your life reactively. This will set you up to be defensive the ENTIRE DAY!

Look, social media is a blessing and a curse. It is such a great tool for many things, but it is THE SINGLE GREATEST TIME SUCKER today! Seriously, have you ever looked at the amount of time you spend on Facebook or Instagram? (Remember, you can check this on your iPhone, a great practice to see how much time you truly do spend on social media). It would be humbling and embarrassing for most of us. If you wake up in the morning and check your social media first thing, you are setting yourself up for failure.

First, you are wasting precious time lying in bed when you could be productive! Second, you are looking at everyone else's PERFECT life that they've portrayed, and you are going to start with the comparison game. "Well, she has this, he does that, their kids are smarter than mine, we need to keep up because they just bought a new car/house," whatever.

STOP!

Comparison is the THIEF of JOY. You are good enough. You are worthy. You can achieve almost anything you want but being on Facebook isn't going to help you do that. Put the phone down.

Chapter 14: The 28-Day Plan

Email

When was the last time that you looked at email in the morning and it gave you a sense of relief? Maybe once, EVER! Usually, it sets you up for frustration. It normally tells you things you don't want to hear. So, instead, put it down! The message is not that important. If it were, they would have called you or text you.

Email is not for emergencies.

But it is a GREAT way to derail your morning. By opening up your email, even for an innocent glance, you are setting yourself to receive a message that is negative and has the potential to reroute or derail your morning—or potentially your whole day. If you wait until you have gone through your morning routine and prepared your mind for the day, then you are more likely to open the email and be productive with it.

The News

The primary job of the news is to get your attention so you will watch more! They want you to stay tuned, so they tease you with information and leave you with cliffhangers. But if you think about it, very rarely are those teasers or headlines positive. A headline that says tomorrow is sunny and 75, leaves you needing very little information. If you get that "headline" then you don't need anything else. Whereas, the headline, "A murderer loose in your town" gets everyone's attention and keeps them glued to the TV/phone for longer.

Look, I'm not saying to bury your head in the sand, but why in the world would you start your day with that? If you instead focused on building a positive mindset, worked to be productive with your morning and then looked at the news, then maybe everything wouldn't be so bad, you could take in the news for what it is–information.

Nightly Recap:

Did you achieve your TOP 3 Actions?

1. _____

2. _____

3. _____

What was good about today?

_____

_____

How did you get better?

_____

_____

Did you drink your water?

_____

CHAPTER 14: THE 28-DAY PLAN

Are you prepared for tomorrow?

_____

Breakfast Prepared [Y] [N]

Lunch Packed [Y] [N]

Tomorrow Morning Wake-Up Time _____

Day 11: Thankful Thursday

Your "Why": _____

Accountability Check-in: _____

Prayer/Devotional/Meditation: (5-10 min.) _____

Bedtime for tonight: _____

What are your TOP 3 Actions of the Day and when will you do them?

1. _____

2. _____

3. _____

How many ounces of water are you going to drink today?

_____

Breakfast: Option 1[Shake] 2[Meal]

Lunch Packed: [Y] [N]

Pack Water Bottle: [Y] [N]

Write five things you are grateful for.

1. _____

2. _____

3. _____

4. _____

5. _____

One person currently:

One person from the past:

Three things that help you in some way:

1. _____

2. _____

3. _____

Nightly Recap:

Did you achieve your TOP 3 Actions?

1. _____

2. _____

3. _____

What was good about today?

_____

_____

How did you get better?

_____

_____

Did you drink your water?

_____

Are you prepared for tomorrow?

_____

Breakfast Prepared [Y] [N]

Lunch Packed [Y] [N]

Tomorrow Morning Wake-Up Time _____

Day 12: Friday Focus

Your "Why": _____

Accountability Check-in: _____

Prayer/Devotional/Meditation: (5-10 min.) _____

Bedtime for tonight: _____

What are your TOP 3 Actions of the Day and when will you do them?

1. _____
2. _____
3. _____

How many ounces of water are you going to drink today?

_____

Breakfast: Option 1[Shake] 2[Meal]

Lunch Packed: [Y] [N]

Pack Water Bottle: [Y] [N]

It's Friday AGAIN!!! Now is the time to set yourself up for success for the weekend. What are your plans for today and this weekend?

Are you traveling?

Do you need to prepare any special meals?

Are you at home?

Do you have any special social plans?

Chapter 14: The 28-Day Plan

Take a few minutes to plan out your weekend so you know exactly where you are going to be and how you can best set yourself up to stay on track.

Nightly Recap:

Did you achieve your TOP 3 Actions?

1. _____

2. _____

3. _____

What was good about today?

_____

_____

How did you get better?

_____

_____

Did you drink your water?

_____

Are you prepared for tomorrow?

_____

Breakfast Prepared [Y] [N]

Lunch Packed [Y] [N]

Tomorrow Morning Wake-Up Time _____

Day 13: Strong Saturday

Your "Why": _____

Accountability Check-in: _____

Prayer/Devotional/Meditation: (5-10 min.) _____

Bedtime for tonight: _____

What are your TOP 3 Actions of the Day and when will you do them?

1. _____

2. _____

3. _____

How many ounces of water are you going to drink today?

_____

Breakfast: Option 1[Shake] 2[Meal]

Lunch Packed: [Y] [N]

Pack Water Bottle: [Y] [N]

What time are you training today?

* Create your shopping list.
* Breakfast for the week
* Cook 2 sets of meals for lunch/snacks
* Plan dinner per day
* Grocery shopping (no spur of the moment purchases)

Nightly Recap:

Did you achieve your TOP 3 Actions?

1. _____

2. _____

3. _____

What was good about today?

_____

_____

How did you get better?

_____

_____

Did you drink your water?

_____

Are you prepared for tomorrow?

_____

Breakfast Prepared [Y] [N]

Lunch Packed [Y] [N]

Tomorrow Morning Wake-Up Time _____

Day 14: Sunday Setup

Your "Why": _____

Prayer/Devotional/Meditation: (5-10 min.) _____

Bedtime for Tonight: _____

How many ounces of water are you going to drink today?

_____

Breakfast: Option 1[Shake] 2[Meal]

Lunch Packed: [Y] [N]

Pack Water Bottle: [Y] [N]

    Sunday should be MOSTLY a day of rest. For many, this is a great time to get a little extra sleep and prepare for the week ahead. Be sure to do something that is good for your soul. Rejuvenate your mind as well as your body.

    Prioritize the important.

Chapter 14: The 28-Day Plan

Take your time during your prep this week to make sure you know when the following will occur.

When will you work out?

* What are the potential roadblocks that can take you off track?
* Family Events
* Date Nights
* What time will you wake up each morning?
* What time will you go to bed?
* What are the five most important things you need to get done this week?

Your calendar is set up! You will be in a GREAT position for the week. Send this to your buddy and/or spouse. Communicate it to others, who can then help you achieve your tasks and hold you accountable to what you said you were going to do!

Nightly Recap:

What was good about today?

_____

_____

How did you get better?

_____

_____

Did you drink your water?

_____

Are you prepared for tomorrow?

_____

Breakfast Prepared [Y] [N]

Lunch Packed [Y] [N]

Tomorrow Morning Wake-Up Time _____

Weekly Prep

Big 5 Actions for the Week:

What are the MOST important things you need to get done this week?

1. _____

2. _____

3. _____

4. _____

5. _____

CHAPTER 14: THE 28-DAY PLAN

Big Calendar Events:

_____

_____

_____

Are your meals ready? [Y] [N]

When will you work out this week? (*The more specific the better.*)

M T W Th F Sa Su

Day 15: Monday Motivation

Self-Accountability Check-In:

Scale: + - previous week

Clothes: Fitting Better Worse or Same as previous week

Mirror: Better Worse or Same as previous week

Energy: Better Worse or Same as previous week

Sleep: Better Worse or Same as previous week

"The only person holding you back is you. No more excuses. It's time to change and take your life to the next level."
-TONY ROBBINS

Be Great Today

Motivational Message: TGIM! Thank God it's Monday! Stop living your life for the weekends. TGIM. Be grateful for this day. Use this as the opportunity to start off the week on a mission.

Your "Why": _____

Accountability Check-in: _____

Prayer/Devotional/Meditation: (5-10 min.) _____

Bedtime for Tonight: _____

What are your TOP 3 Actions of the Day and when will you do them?

1. _____

2. _____

3. _____

How many ounces of water are you going to drink today?

_____

Breakfast: Option 1[Shake] 2[Meal]

Lunch Packed: [Y] [N]

Pack Water Bottle: [Y] [N]

Follow the schedule.

* Eat the meals you made
* Train when you said you would

Chapter 14: The 28-Day Plan

* Get up when you said you would
* Go to bed when you said you would

Just follow the plan. Revisit your why. You are set up for success. Now, go do it!

Nightly Recap:

Did you achieve your TOP 3 Actions?

1. _____

2. _____

3. _____

What was good about today?

_____

_____

How did you get better?

_____

_____

Did you drink your water?

_____

Are you prepared for tomorrow?

_____

Breakfast Prepared [Y] [N]

Lunch Packed [Y] [N]

Tomorrow Morning Wake-Up Time _____

Day 16: Transformation Tuesday

Your "Why": _____

Accountability Check-in: _____

Prayer/Devotional/Meditation: (5-10 min.) _____

Bedtime for tonight: _____

What are your TOP 3 Actions of the Day and when will you do them?

1. _____
2. _____
3. _____

How many ounces of water are you going to drink today?

_____

Breakfast: Option 1[Shake] 2[Meal]

Lunch Packed: [Y] [N]

Pack Water Bottle: [Y] [N]

Chapter 14: The 28-Day Plan

Transformation begins in the mind. Make sure today that you keep your goals and priorities in front of you! Today, we are going to focus on statements around your career. Let's focus your brain around statements that will lift and affirm the work you are doing.

I am living my best life.

I have to forgive myself.

I further my career with every decision I make at work.

I am enthusiastic about the work I do.

Nightly Recap:

Did you achieve your TOP 3 Actions?

1. _____
2. _____
3. _____

What was good about today?

_____

_____

How did you get better?

_____

_____

Did you drink your water?

_____

Are you prepared for tomorrow?

_____

Breakfast Prepared [Y] [N]

Lunch Packed [Y] [N]

Tomorrow Morning Wake-Up Time _____

Day 17: Wednesday Work

Your "Why": _____

Accountability Check-in: _____

Prayer/Devotional/Meditation: (5-10 min.) _____

Bedtime for tonight: _____

What are your TOP 3 Actions of the Day and when will you do them?

1. _____

2. _____

3. _____

Chapter 14: The 28-Day Plan

How many ounces of water are you going to drink today?

_____

Breakfast: Option 1[Shake] 2[Meal]

Lunch Packed: [Y] [N]

Pack Water Bottle: [Y] [N]

<u>Rules for Life</u>

What are the five–ten things that you want to be true about your life? Think about WHO you want to be and what would it take to make that part of who you are. We CANNOT keep ourselves accountable without rules.

Think of a being at a party. You are one week into your new lifestyle plan and the host offers you something DELICIOUS looking to eat. "No thanks, I've made a lifestyle change and I don't eat that way anymore."

But your friend keeps after you. "Are you SURE you don't want a slice, just a small one? Come on, it's just one!"

Do you cave? Do you fold to the pressure?

Most of us don't have hard rules in place or don't think about what we are going to do at a party in advance because we haven't made a promise to ourselves. That's all rules are—a promise to that we made a commitment to our health, so we are going to keep it.

You established some rules for yourself with your bed time and wake-up time already. Now it's time to think bigger and plan out some true statements that we will make our Rules for Life.

Think through the following. What are your rules for:

* Drinking Alcohol [Y] [N]

    If yes, how often and how much?

* Eating

    When will you eat each day?

    Eating Out:

    How often

    Splurge or Stay on Plan?

    Eating at Parties:

    Eat before

    Splurge or Stay on Plan?

* When will you leave work to go home?
* When time do you get to work?
* Do you put your phone away when you get home?

We know that there will be a need to have flexibility at times, but that is the exception rather than the rule. If you create more structure, you will have more freedom. The more you work to organize your life, the easier it will be to adapt when you have to change your plans.

Chapter 14: The 28-Day Plan

So, begin creating rules for your life based on the principles that matter most to you.

Nightly Recap:

Did you achieve your TOP 3 Actions?

1. _____

2. _____

3. _____

What was good about today?

_____

_____

How did you get better?

_____

_____

Did you drink your water?

_____

Are you prepared for tomorrow?

_____

Breakfast Prepared [Y] [N]

Lunch Packed [Y] [N]

Tomorrow Morning Wake-Up Time _____

Day 18: Thankful Thursday

Your "Why": _____

Accountability Check-in: _____

Prayer/Devotional/Meditation: (5-10 min.) _____

Bedtime for tonight: _____

What are your TOP 3 Actions of the Day and when will you do them?

1. _____

2. _____

3. _____

How many ounces of water are you going to drink today?

_____

Breakfast: Option 1[Shake] 2[Meal]

Lunch Packed: [Y] [N]

Pack Water Bottle: [Y] [N]

Chapter 14: The 28-Day Plan

Write down five people/things you are grateful for:

_____

_____

_____

No matter what your scenario or circumstance, there is always something for which to be grateful. Make sure to include the people in your life that make or have made a difference, the body that you have and how it works, the career or job that you have/school that you go to. If you are lacking in any one of those areas, great. Find something else. If you don't have a job, be grateful for the opportunity to go GET ONE. An attitude of gratitude will CHANGE your perspective and make your life way more productive and filled with good things.

Nightly Recap:

Did you achieve your TOP 3 Actions?

1. _____

2. _____

3. _____

What was good about today?

_____

BE GREAT TODAY

How did you get better?

Did you drink your water?

Are you prepared for tomorrow?

Breakfast Prepared [Y] [N]

Lunch Packed [Y] [N]

Tomorrow Morning Wake-Up Time _____

Day 19: Friday Focus

Your "Why": _____

Accountability Check-in: _____

Prayer/Devotional/Meditation: (5-10 min.) _____

Bedtime for tonight: _____

Chapter 14: The 28-Day Plan

What are your TOP 3 Actions of the Day and when will you do them?

1. _____

2. _____

3. _____

How many ounces of water are you going to drink today?

_____

Breakfast: Option 1[Shake] 2[Meal]

Lunch Packed: [Y] [N]

Pack Water Bottle: [Y] [N]

Don't let this weekend be the one that throws you off.

We've established your rules for life on Wednesday, NOW is the perfect time to implement them!

Focus on:

- Knowing where you are going to be
- What temptations WILL come up
- Stick to your rules

What is the BIGGEST thing you need to DO in order to set yourself up for success today and going into the weekend? Think through the following.

Are you traveling?

* What will it take to travel well?

    Food/Snacks/Water

* How can you stay on track with your workouts/training?

    Hotel/ Running/Friends…

Are you going to be home?

* Do you have tasks/ chores to do to set you up for the week ahead?
* Are you behind on the work you need to do at home?
* What are you going to do to prevent overeating or eating out?

Did you talk to your buddy about this weekend?

Nightly Recap:

Did you achieve your TOP 3 Actions?

1. _____

2. _____

3. _____

What was good about today?

_____

_____

How did you get better?

_____

Did you drink your water?

_____

Are you prepared for tomorrow?

_____

Breakfast Prepared [Y] [N]

Lunch Packed [Y] [N]

Tomorrow Morning Wake-Up Time _____

Day 20: Strong Saturday

Your "Why": _____

Accountability Check-in: _____

Prayer/Devotional/Meditation: (5-10 min.) _____

Bedtime for tonight: _____

BE GREAT TODAY

What are your TOP 3 Actions of the Day and when will you do them?

1. _____

2. _____

3. _____

How many ounces of water are you going to drink today?

_____

Breakfast: Option 1[Shake] 2[Meal]

Lunch Packed: [Y] [N]

Pack Water Bottle: [Y] [N]

* Create your shopping list
* Breakfast for the week
* Cook two sets of meals for lunch/snacks
* Plan dinner per day
* Grocery shopping (no spur of the moment purchases)

Nightly Recap:

Did you achieve your TOP 3 Actions?

1. _____

2. _____

3. _____

What was good about today?

_____

_____

How did you get better?

_____

_____

Did you drink your water?

_____

Are you prepared for tomorrow?

_____

Breakfast Prepared [Y] [N]

Lunch Packed [Y] [N]

Tomorrow Morning Wake-Up Time _____

Day 21: Sunday Setup

Your "Why": _____

Accountability Check-in: _____

Be Great Today

Prayer/Devotional/Meditation: (5-10 min.) _____

Bedtime for tonight: _____

What are your TOP 3 Actions of the Day and when will you do them?

1. _____
2. _____
3. _____

How many ounces of water are you going to drink today?

_____

Breakfast: Option 1[Shake] 2[Meal]

Lunch Packed: [Y] [N]

Pack Water Bottle: [Y] [N]

Sunday should be MOSTLY a day of rest. For many, this is a great time to get a little extra sleep and prepare for the week ahead. Be sure to do something that is good for your soul. Rejuvenate your mind as well as your body.

Prioritize the important.

Take your time during your prep this week to make sure you know when the following will occur:

When will you work out?

Chapter 14: The 28-Day Plan

- * What are the potential roadblocks that can take you off track?
- * Family Events
- * Date Nights
- * What time will you wake up each morning?
- * What time will you go to bed?
- * What are the five most important things you need to get done this week?

Your calendar is set up!

You will be in a GREAT position for the week.

Send this to your buddy and/or spouse.

Communicate it to others, who can then help you achieve your tasks and hold you accountable to what you said you were going to do!

Nightly Recap:

Did you achieve your TOP 3 Actions?

1. _____
2. _____
3. _____

BE GREAT TODAY

What was good about today?

_____

_____

How did you get better?

_____

_____

Did you drink your water?

_____

Are you prepared for tomorrow?

_____

Breakfast Prepared [Y] [N]

Lunch Packed [Y] [N]

Tomorrow Morning Wake-Up Time _____

CHAPTER 14: THE 28-DAY PLAN

Weekly Prep:

Big 5 Actions for the Week:

What are the MOST important things you need to get done this week?

1. _____

2. _____

3. _____

4. _____

5. _____

Big Calendar Events:

_____

_____

_____

Are your meals ready? [Y] [N]

When will you work out this week? (*The more specific the better.*)

M T W Th F Sa Su

Day 22: Monday Motivation

Self-Accountability Check-In:

Scale: + - previous week

Clothes: Fitting Better Worse or Same as previous week

Mirror: Better Worse or Same as previous week

Energy: Better Worse or Same as previous week

Sleep: Better Worse or Same as previous week

> *"I fear not the man that has practiced 10,000 kicks one time, but I fear the man that has practiced one kick 10,000 times."*
> — BRUCE LEE

Motivational Message: You have worked so hard to build these great rhythms in your life, keep working on them. Every day is an opportunity to move closer to the best version of yourself. Keep your eyes focused on doing your best and following your rules for life and pursuing greatness. Repetition is the key to progress.

Your "Why": _____

Accountability Check-in: _____

Prayer/Devotional/Meditation: (5-10 min.) _____

Bedtime for Tonight: _____

Chapter 14: The 28-Day Plan

What are your TOP 3 Actions of the Day and when will you do them?

1. _____

2. _____

3. _____

How many ounces of water are you going to drink today?

_____

Breakfast: Option 1[Shake] 2[Meal]

Lunch Packed: [Y] [N]

Pack Water Bottle: [Y] [N]

You are on a mission this week. You have been cultivating new habits, developing new ways of living, working and maximizing your potential. You know your why. You know exactly what you need to do today. Go do what you said you were going to do.

Follow the schedule.

* The Food is ready

   Eat the meals you made

* Train when you scheduled it

   Train when you said you would

* Wake up on purpose

   Get up when you said you would

* Set up tomorrow by going to bed on time.
Go to bed when you said you would

Nightly Recap:

Did you achieve your TOP 3 Actions?

1. _____

2. _____

3. _____

What was good about today?

_____

_____

How did you get better?

_____

_____

Did you drink your water?

_____

Are you prepared for tomorrow?

_____

Breakfast Prepared [Y] [N]

Lunch Packed [Y] [N]

Tomorrow Morning Wake-Up Time _____

Day 23: Transformation Tuesday

Your "Why": _____

Accountability Check-in: _____

Prayer/Devotional/Meditation: (5-10 min.) _____

Bedtime for tonight: _____

What are your TOP 3 Actions of the Day and when will you do them?

1. _____
2. _____
3. _____

How many ounces of water are you going to drink today?

_____

Breakfast: Option 1[Shake] 2[Meal]

Lunch Packed: [Y] [N]

Pack Water Bottle: [Y] [N]

Today, we are going to write three statements that are focused on our love. Whether they are focused on faith, your spouse, partner, kids or family, write statements about the love in your life.

* I am loving and loveable.
* My words are loving and uplifting to everyone I meet.
* I wake up every day filled with joy for my life.

Nightly Recap:

Did you achieve your TOP 3 Actions?

1. _____
2. _____
3. _____

What was good about today?

_____

_____

How did you get better?

_____

_____

Chapter 14: The 28-Day Plan

🍶 Did you drink your water?

_____

Are you prepared for tomorrow?

_____

Breakfast Prepared [Y] [N]

Lunch Packed [Y] [N]

Tomorrow Morning Wake-Up Time _____

Day 24: Wednesday Work

Your "Why": _____

Accountability Check-in: _____

Prayer/Devotional/Meditation: (5-10 min.) _____

Bedtime for tonight: _____

What are your TOP 3 Actions of the Day and when will you do them?

1. _____

2. _____

3. _____

Be Great Today

How many ounces of water are you going to drink today?

_____

Breakfast: Option 1[Shake] 2[Meal]

Lunch Packed: [Y] [N]

Pack Water Bottle: [Y] [N]

Take Full Responsibility for your life.

Own Everything.

When we blame others, situations or circumstances, we give our power away. You are no longer in control and we allow others to dictate OUR lives.

You have more power than you think.

Take responsibility for everything. The good, the bad, and everything else.

Stop living a life that is reactive instead of proactive. You established rules for your life to make sure that you don't allow others to take you off course. You have the ability to dictate the terms of your life. Be strong. You are capable of achieving almost any goal that you have. Focus your attention on your goals. Write it down. Own Your Calendar. Be present in every moment.

If you fall short of a goal, GOOD! It's an opportunity to learn. Focus on the process. Pick a target and reach for it. Evaluate the gap and act to overcome it. Repeat.

Obstacles ARE the Path. Keep moving forward. Find solutions to new problems.

You can do this!

What do you need to change or take responsibility for?

Are there specific actions that you need to continue to change and adapt in order to reach the best version of yourself?

Do you need to change your attitude about a person in your life?

Do you need to change your attitude about an event or activity in your life?

Think through where you can take ownership of your attitudes and actions to make your vision for your life come true.

Nightly Recap:

Did you achieve your TOP 3 Actions?

1. _____

2. _____

3. _____

What was good about today?

_____

_____

How did you get better?

_____

💧 Did you drink your water?

_____

Are you prepared for tomorrow?

_____

Breakfast Prepared [Y] [N]

Lunch Packed [Y] [N]

Tomorrow Morning Wake-Up Time _____

Day 25: Thankful Thursday

Your "Why": _____

Accountability Check-in: _____

Prayer/Devotional/Meditation: (5-10 min.) _____

Bedtime for tonight: _____

What are your TOP 3 Actions of the Day and when will you do them?

1. _____

2. _____

Chapter 14: The 28-Day Plan

3. _____

How many ounces of water are you going to drink today?

_____

Breakfast: Option 1[Shake] 2[Meal]

Lunch Packed: [Y] [N]

Pack Water Bottle: [Y] [N]

Write three-five people that you are thankful for who have had a huge influence in your life and may not currently be present. It is good to reflect on people who impacted you. It will help you to remember lessons they taught you and remind you of a time in your life where you were going through a struggle or challenge and how you got through it. Or maybe it will cause you to remember a time of celebration and how someone walked with you through that.

Nightly Recap:

Did you achieve your TOP 3 Actions?

1. _____

2. _____

3. _____

What was good about today?

_____

How did you get better?

_____

_____

Did you drink your water?

_____

Are you prepared for tomorrow?

_____

Breakfast Prepared [Y] [N]

Lunch Packed [Y] [N]

Tomorrow Morning Wake-Up Time _____

Day 26: Friday Focus

Your "Why": _____

Accountability Check-in: _____

Prayer/Devotional/Meditation: (5-10 min.) _____

Bedtime for tonight: _____

Chapter 14: The 28-Day Plan

What are your TOP 3 Actions of the Day and when will you do them?

1. _____

2. _____

3. _____

How many ounces of water are you going to drink today?

_____

Breakfast: Option 1[Shake] 2[Meal]

Lunch Packed: [Y] [N]

Pack Water Bottle: [Y] [N]

You have worked HARD this week! You put in the time and effort to follow your rules: eat well, exercise and focus on what is important. Today and the upcoming weekend are NO DIFFERENT.

Reaffirm your rules. Know what you are going to do. We often fall off on the weekend because we are less structured than normal. Be disciplined. Know the WHY, WHAT, WHEN and HOW of your weekend!

You are in control!

Are you traveling?

* What will it take to travel well?

Food/Snacks/Water

* How can you stay on track with your workouts/training?

   Hotel/ Running/Friends...

Are you going to be home?

* Do you have tasks/chores to do to set you up for the week ahead?
* Are you behind on the work you need to do at home?
* What are you going to do to prevent overeating or eating out?

Did you talk to your buddy about this weekend?

Nightly Recap:

Did you achieve your TOP 3 Actions?

1. _____
2. _____
3. _____

What was good about today?

_____

How did you get better?

_____

_____

🚰 Did you drink your water?

_____

Are you prepared for tomorrow?

_____

Breakfast Prepared [Y] [N]

Lunch Packed [Y] [N]

Tomorrow Morning Wake-Up Time _____

Day 27: Strong Saturday

Your "Why": _____

Accountability Check-in: _____

Prayer/Devotional/Meditation: (5-10 min.) _____

Bedtime for tonight: _____

What are your TOP 3 Actions of the Day and when will you do them?

1. _____
2. _____
3. _____

How many ounces of water are you going to drink today?

_____

Breakfast: Option 1[Shake] 2[Meal]

Lunch Packed: [Y] [N]

Pack Water Bottle: [Y] [N]

* Create your shopping list.
* Breakfast for the week
* Cook two sets of meals for lunch/snacks
* Plan dinner per day
* Grocery shopping (no spur of the moment purchases)

Nightly Recap:

Did you achieve your TOP 3 Actions?

1. _____

2. _____

3. _____

What was good about today?

_____

How did you get better?

_____

🥤 Did you drink your water?

Are you prepared for tomorrow?

Breakfast Prepared [Y] [N]

Lunch Packed [Y] [N]

Tomorrow Morning Wake-Up Time _____

Day 28: Sunday Setup

Your "Why": _____

Accountability Check-in: _____

Prayer/Devotional/Meditation: (5-10 min.) _____

Bedtime for tonight: _____

What are your TOP 3 Actions of the Day and when will you do them?

1. _____

2. _____

3. _____

How many ounces of water are you going to drink today?

_____

Breakfast: Option 1[Shake] 2[Meal]

Lunch Packed: [Y] [N]

Pack Water Bottle: [Y] [N]

Sunday should be MOSTLY a day of rest. For many, this is a great time to get a little extra sleep and prepare for the week ahead. Be sure to do something that is good for your soul. Rejuvenate your mind as well as your body.

Prioritize the important.

Take your time during your prep this week to make sure you know when the following will occur.

When will you work out?

* What are the potential roadblocks that can take you off track?
* Family Events
* Date Nights
* What time will you wake up each morning?
* What time will you go to bed?
* What are the five most important things you need to get done this week?

Chapter 14: The 28-Day Plan

Your calendar is set up!

You will be in a GREAT position for the week.

Send this to your buddy and/or spouse.

Communicate it to others, who can then help you achieve your tasks and hold you accountable to what you said you were going to do!

Nightly Recap:

Did you achieve your TOP 3 Actions?

1. _____

2. _____

3. _____

What was good about today?

_____

How did you get better?

 Did you drink your water?

_____

Are you prepared for tomorrow?

_____

Breakfast Prepared [Y] [N]

Lunch Packed [Y] [N]

Tomorrow Morning Wake-Up Time _____

Weekly Prep

Big 5 Actions for the Week:

What are the MOST important things you need to get done this week?

1. _____
2. _____
3. _____
4. _____
5. _____

Big Calendar Events:

_____

_____

_____

Are your meals ready? [Y] [N]

CHAPTER 14: THE 28-DAY PLAN

When will you work out this week? (*The more specific the better.*)

M T W Th F Sa Su

Day 29 and Beyond!

This is not the END! This is just the beginning! You have worked SO HARD to build patterns into your life that will lead you to make real, sustainable changes in order to live YOUR BEST life! Be Intentional each and every day so that you can achieve your goals. As my friend and mentor, Todd Durkin, says, "Live a life worth telling a story about," and don't forget, as always, to Be Great Today!

Join us at www.begreattodaybook.com.

Motivational Quotes

"WHAT YOU KNOW RIGHT NOW IS ENOUGH TO GET YOU STARTED ON SOMETHING BIG."
—Michael Hyatt

"IF YOU ALWAYS DO WHAT YOU'VE ALWAYS DONE, YOU ALWAYS GET WHAT YOU'VE ALWAYS GOTTEN."
—Jessie Potter

"IT DOESN'T MATTER HOW SLOW YOU GO AS LONG AS YOU DO NOT STOP."
—Confucius

"WE CANNOT DO EVERYTHING AT ONCE, BUT WE CAN DO SOMETHING AT ONCE."
—Calvin Coolidge

"WITH ORDINARY TALENT AND EXTRAORDINARY PERSEVERANCE, ALL THINGS ARE ATTAINABLE."
—Thomas Fowell Buxton

"TO JOURNEY WITHOUT DIRECTION IS WASTED EFFORT."
—St. Mark the Ascetic

Chapter 14: The 28-Day Plan

"IF AT FIRST YOU DON'T SUCCEED, YOU'RE NORMAL."
—Michael Hyatt

"DREAMS DON'T WORK UNLESS YOU DO."
—John C. Maxwell

"WHEN THERE IS A HILL TO CLIMB, DON'T THINK THAT WAITING WILL MAKE IT SMALLER."
—Unknown

"OBSTACLES ARE THOSE FRIGHTFUL THINGS YOU SEE WHEN YOU TAKE YOUR EYES OFF YOUR GOAL."
—Henry Ford

"THE DIFFERENCE BETWEEN SUCCESSFUL PEOPLE AND VERY SUCCESSFUL PEOPLE IS THAT THE VERY SUCCESSFUL PEOPLE SAY NO TO ALMOST EVERYTHING."
—Warren Buffett

"INSIGHT WITHOUT ACTION IS WORTHLESS."
—Marie Forleo

"EVERY YES MUST BE DEFENDED WITH A THOUSAND NO'S."
—Jeff Walker

"LACK OF DIRECTION, NOT LACK OF TIME, IS THE PROBLEM. WE ALL HAVE 24-HOUR DAYS."
—Zig Ziglar

"YESTERDAY IS HISTORY, TOMORROW IS A MYSTERY, TODAY IS A GIFT, THAT'S WHY IT'S CALLED THE PRESENT."
—Unknown

"I FEAR NOT THE MAN THAT HAS PRACTICED 10,000 KICKS ONE TIME, BUT I FEAR THE MAN THAT HAS PRACTICED ONE KICK 10,000 TIMES."
—Bruce Lee

BE GREAT TODAY!

Acknowledgments

I have so much to be grateful for in my life.

I am thankful for the grace, peace and salvation that I have received through my Lord and Savior Jesus Christ. My faith is an instrumental part of my life, the guiding light, and my decision to follow him in 2001 at Northwoods Church in Peoria, Illinois has forever changed who I am.

To my wife, **Theresa**, there aren't enough words to describe my thanks to you. You are my best friend, the one I love and my support. You make me a better person. Thank you for choosing to go on this ride of a life with me. I Love You.

To my boys, Riley, Cooper and Colton

Riley—You inspire me to love better and help others more. I love that you are a Cardinals crazy, a history buff and that you have a heart for Jesus and other people. I can't wait to see who you become.

Chapter 14: Acknowledgments

Cooper—Your imagination inspires me to dream more and write more. Your love of writing was a catalyst for me to write this book! I can't wait to see how many books you publish. They are going to be great! You are going to do great things for GOD in this world!

Colton—I love your big attitude and smile. I am so glad I get to be your daddy. May you always hit the ball far and hard. May your spirit never be tamed, and may you become all that GOD created you to be.

Mom and **Dad, Geri** and **Tony Kegley**—Thank you for your love and hard work to give me the opportunity to pursue the things that I love. I am grateful for your sacrifice and generosity of time and resources.

To my sisters Sara Gilpin and Katelyn Tassart—

Sara—Thanks for not picking up the spoon ;). I am so grateful you are my sister. Thank you for being such a great aunt and sister-in-law to Theresa.

Chad- Thanks for being a great brother in law! I am grateful that you are apart of our family!

Alexis, Zachary, Makayla, Nicholas and Quentin—Being your uncle has been such a joy. I hope you are able to achieve all you desire.

Kate—I hope your new adventure is filled with joy. I can't wait to come visit. Love you, kid.

JJ- Thanks for loving my sister. May the Arizona sun shine light into your life.

My mother- and father-in-law, **Mark and Jan Schleder** —Thank you for opening your arms and family to me. You have always treated me like one of your own, and I am grateful for your example and love.

Leanne Walton—I am so grateful for all your support, encouragement and prayers over the years. Thanks for being such an awesome sister and chiropractor.

Dan Walton—Thanks for being a brother. I always enjoy our time together. You are an inspiration in your faith, as a father and husband.

Caleb Schleder—To my little brother. Some of my favorite memories from the Canary House involve you, the trampoline and Tony Hawk. Proud of who you have become and excited to see what's ahead.

Jordan Schleder—So grateful you are a part of our family. Thanks for taking care of Caleb and being a great aunt to our boys!

Coach Pat Taphorn—I got the rebound. I have never forgotten that lesson. Thanks for being an example of faith, family, fitness (sports). I am so grateful to you and Lisa for being a part of some formative years of my life.

Chapter 14: Acknowledgments

Randy Shafer—You may be gone my friend, but I am so grateful for you. Without you, I wouldn't know Jesus the way I do. You treated me with an exceptional love that was weird to me at the time, but now I know was given by someone who truly loved Jesus. I miss you, my friend, can't wait to get one of your big hugs in heaven.

Marnie Dick—Thanks for being a great friend in a tough time in my life. Your friendship was huge and your invitation to Northwoods Community Church forever changed my life. Thank you!

Todd Durkin—You are a hero to me. You have inspired so many. I am so glad that I bought the IMPACT Body Plan so many years ago and then followed you at Perform Better. Thank you for stepping outside of the walls of Fitness Quest 10 and creating the Mastermind. It has changed my life. You are the real deal. Thank you!

Frank Pucher—Coach, thanks for always bringing me back to center. You keep me from chasing to many shiny things. You are wise and a great encouragement to me. Thanks for leading team Do Better!

My Movement Fitness Team:

Liz Lopez—Your growth is tremendous and encouraging. Thanks for not wasting $49. It certainly has worked out for us!

Matt Cotton—You continue to grow and challenge yourself. Thanks for leading our younger athletes and being willing to step into any spot we need. You have a bright future in this industry.

Cheri White—Thanks for being a friend to Theresa and me first and now a part of our staff. Your tenacity is a blessing, and I can't wait to see how you continue to develop in this role. You are a teacher, encourager and motivator. Fit Kids is going to be amazing!

Nick Miramontes—You are a soldier. I am so grateful for your willingness to help in any capacity and use your expertise to help make sure people move well and stay healthy.

Austin Alexander—You have made a huge impact on our team in a short time. Your entertaining and intentional personality make people feel both comfortable and cared for at the same time. You are going to be a great Physical Therapist!

David Black—To our partner, thanks for pushing us to step out and take a chance.

Kelli Watson and Greg Justice (Scriptor Publishing)—Thank you for believing in my message and supporting my dream to write a book. I could not have done this without you!

Ryan Morse—Thanks for your support and accountability to start this year! I am encouraged by our conversations and watching you grow.

Chapter 14: Acknowledgments

Andrew Simpson—Thanks for being willing to speak truth, but give hope at the same time. I am encouraged by what you are doing and who you are.

Team TD1: Team Do Better—You all continually call out the best in me and push me to grow my business, but also to become a better version of myself. Your vulnerability and willingness to help are encouraging and challenging to me at the same time!

TD Mastermind: You are the best of the best. A group of fire breathing dragons that inspire and motivate me to continue to grow and get better. Thank you for all of your contributions to my life and business!

To the {815}! We were supposed to live here for 18 months or less. It's now been 12 years and we could not be more grateful for all of our friends that have adopted us and helped us make Rockford home.

There is no way I could thank everyone that has had an impact on me. I am so grateful to you for buying this book! Thanks, and Be Great Today!

Made in the USA
Columbia, SC
09 April 2019